ADA – A SHEFFIELD LASS

Ada Bramhall, born in Sheffield in 1920, was descended on the one side from one of the more affluent families in the Sheffield area – the Waterfalls - and on the other - one of the poorest – the Bramhalls. She never benefitted from any of the wealth and success of the Waterfalls but endured the poverty and deprivation suffered by the Bramhalls in the 20's and 30's.

JOHN WATERFALL 1745 - 1803	GEORGE BRAMHALL 1764 -1842
(wife Martha 1755 - 1810)	(wife unknown)
I	I
STEPHEN WATERFALL 1784 - 1859	GEORGE BRAMHALL 1794 - 1878
(wife Mary 1789 - 1866)	(wife Hannah 1800 -1883)
I	I
JAMES WATERFALL 1813 - 1877	JOHN BRAMHALL 1826 - 1870
(wife Sarah 1813 - 1900)	(wife Ann 1829 - 1858)
I	I
HENRY WATERFALL 1837 - 1896	JOHN BRAMHALL 1852 - 1910
(wife Betsy 1828 - 1893)	(wife Martha 1852 - 1913)
I	I
RICHARD MILES WATERFALL 1874 - 1944	ANN ELIZABETH BRAMHALL 1873 - 1933
I	I
FLORENCE BRAMHALL 1893 - 1976	FLORENCE BRAMHALL 1893 - 1976
I	I
ADA BRAMHALL 1920 - 2007	ADA BRAMHALL 1920 - 2007

The Waterfalls were a large family, heavily involved in file manufacturing and mainly resident in the Fulwood and Crookes area of Sheffield.

John Waterfall born in 1745 had moved to Sheffield from Derbyshire at the age of 26 and worked as a filesmith, marrying Martha Corbridge, aged just 16. They had 6 children, including 2 sons, who also became filesmiths, with manufacturing businesses of their own, employing several workers.

Their youngest son Stephen born in 1784, married Mary Crownshaw - their first son James was born in 1813, a further seven children being born between 1815 and 1829.

When James was 23 and already a successful file manufacturer, he married Sarah Woodhead Marshall, the daughter of a farmer from Stannington who held the lease of Fulwood Hall.

Their first-born son Henry (Ada's great grandfather) was born in 1837 at Whitley Wood, Ecclesall, and by 1841 the family were living at Nether Green – parents Stephen and Mary lived nearby at Heald House, Carsick Hill Road.

By 1851, Stephen was a file manufacturer employing 5 men, and all the rest of the family were involved in the same industry. Son George was a filesmith, son William a file forger, and sons Alfred and Samuel were file cutters. It is not known whether the sons were employees of their father, but George, William and Alfred all went on to become file manufacturers in their own right.

At the same time, their eldest son James was a file and cutlery manufacturer, employing 9 men, and resident at Ran Moor.

The Waterfalls were now respected and influential persons in the area and became involved in local politics.

In June 1851, according to a letter sent to the Sheffield Independent, there was a meeting to discuss candidates for Town Councillor for Upper Hallam.

The letter, from a Mr Rhodes, stated that he had called a few friends together to consider asking a Mr Hoole to stand as candidate for the Town Councillor of the Upper Hallam ward. While they were discussing the merits of different persons, "Mr *James Waterfall came into the room. He had not been invited.*" The letter went on to suggest that there were some underhand tactics by James Waterfall, to enable the election of a Mr Parker, the candidate preferred by Isaac Ironside, Town Councillor for Ecclesall. It appeared that Mr Parker had not paid rates for long enough to be entitled to be on the burgess roll, so was barred. A second candidate, a Mr Roper, was also supported by Isaac Ironside and another member of his family but was not successful in being elected. The letter went on to say that "*The burgesses of Upper Hallam, by their votes on*

Monday last, have freed themselves from the tyrannical dictation of the Ironsides."

Isaac Ironside was a supporter of Chartism, speaking alongside Ebenezer Elliott at mass meetings in Sheffield. He was a founder member of the Mechanics' Institute but was removed from his post as honorary secretary after placing eight books concerning socialism on the shelves. He supported women's suffrage and encouraged the founding of the Sheffield Female Political Association. He also helped to establish the model workhouse farm at Hollow Meadows. In 1851, he founded the Sheffield Free Press and corresponded with Karl Marx.

It would appear from this that James Waterfall was politically minded, with Socialist beliefs and ideas. If he was a Chartist, he supported the following aims of the Chartist movement: -

- Every man over 21 to have the right to vote
- A secret ballot to be introduced
- A MP did not have to own property of a certain value or above to become a MP
- All MPs to be paid to allow working men to serve in Parliament
- All constituencies to be equal in terms of population size
- Elections to Parliament to be held every year so that MPs would have to answer to their voters if they had not performed well.

Before the Reform Act of 1832, only large landowners could vote. After 1832, only male occupants in houses valued at £10 per year were entitled to vote. Women were excluded completely but, in 1869, single and widowed rate paying women were given the right to vote for municipal councils, but not in parliamentary elections.

The Waterfall family, fathers, sons, brothers, and cousins were keen sportsmen, mainly taking part in cricket and football matches in the Hallam area.

Sheffield Football Club, the world's oldest football club, was founded in 1857 by Nathaniel Creswick and William Prest, and offered membership to "gentlemen", consisting mainly of the elite of the town and neighbourhood. Most of the members were Collegians, that is, old boys of the Sheffield Collegiate School, which was founded in 1836 in new buildings on the corner of Ecclesall Road and Collegiate Crescent

Two members of Sheffield Football Club, Thomas Vickers and John Charles Shaw (married to James Waterfall's daughter), decided to establish a club that was not as exclusive as the Sheffield Football Club, and went on to found the Hallam Football Club in 1860. This was the beginning of a fierce rivalry between the two clubs and on 29th December 1862, William Waterfall, aged 38, made the local news, but for the wrong reasons.

Sheffield FC was playing Hallam FC in a football

game at Bramall Lane, in aid of the Lancashire Distress Fund. The Lancashire Cotton Famine, (1861–65), was a depression in the textile industry brought about by the interruption of cotton imports caused by the American Civil War. The factories ran out of raw cotton to process, large parts of Lancashire region's working society became unemployed, and went from being the most prosperous workers in Britain to the most impoverished. Local relief committees were set up, and appeals were made for money both locally and nationally.

It was one of the first-ever football games to be recorded in a newspaper. The Sheffield Independent Newspaper reported that: -

" *The Hallam party, having won the toss, played with the wind in their favour, but at half-time, having failed to score, the ends were changed.*
After a rest of 15 minutes, play was resumed. The great expectation seemed to be that Sheffield, with the wind now in their favour, would soon get a goal. The Hallam men, however, played with great determination and successfully defended their goal. They appeared to have many partisans present and when they succeeded in "downing" a man, their ardent friends were more noisily jubilant.
At one time it appeared that the match would be turned into a general fight. Major Creswick (Sheffield) had got the ball away and was struggling against

*great odds - Mr Shaw and Mr Waterfall (of Hallam).
Major Creswick was held by Waterfall and in the
struggle, Waterfall was accidentally hit by the Major.
All parties agreed that the hit was accidental.
Waterfall, however, ran at the Major in the most
irritable manner, and struck him several times. He
also threw off his waistcoat and began to show fight
in earnest. Major Creswick, who preserved his
temper admirably, did not return a single blow.
They were surrounded by partisans and for a few
minutes there was every appearance of a general
fight amongst players and spectators. The advice of
older and cooler heads at length prevailed, the field
was cleared and play again resumed. At 3 o'clock the
play terminated in a "draw".
The conduct of Waterfall was much condemned and
several of the Hallam players expressed their deep
regret at the occurrence. There were a few, however,
who seemed to rejoice that the Major had been hit.
The cry was very general that Waterfall should be
expelled from the field, but, though this extreme
course was not taken, he was quietly placed as
goalkeeper for the short time the play continued."*

However, the following week, a letter appeared in
The Sheffield Independent defending the actions of
William Waterfall:

*"The unfair report in your paper of the... football
match played on the Bramall Lane ground between
the Sheffield and Hallam Football Clubs calls for a
hearing from the other side. We have nothing to say
about the result - there was no score - but to defend*

7

the character and behaviour of our respected player, Mr William Waterfall, by detailing the facts as they occurred between him and Major Creswick. In the early part of the game, Waterfall charged the Major, on which the Major threatened to strike him if he did so again. Later in the game, when all the players were waiting a decision of the umpires, the Major, very unfairly, took the ball from the hands of one of our players and commenced kicking it towards their goal. He was met by Waterfall who charged him and the Major struck Waterfall on the face, which Waterfall immediately returned."

In 1861, James Waterfall, aged 48, file manager, and wife Sarah aged 47, were living at 4 Cliff View, Ranmoor, with son Henry aged 23, also a file manager, daughter Ann aged 21, son Robert aged 17, a file cutter, and daughters Elizabeth aged 12, Anne Marie aged 9 and Florence aged 4.

Cliff View, 376 Fulwood Road, is now the West 10 restaurant.

On 14th April 1864, Henry Waterfall, manufacturer, married Betsy Rose Miles in the Parish Church at Edgbaston, Warwickshire (now part of Birmingham). Betsy's father Richard Miles was quite well off when he died in 1865 - his estate was about £4000 – a decent amount in those days and worth £440,000 today.

In his will, dated 30th December 1864, i.e. 8 months after Henry Waterfall's marriage to Betsy, he specified that money bequeathed to any females in his will should "be held by them independently of any husband". Did he have an idea of Henry's future money problems?

Henry and Betsy may have lived for a time in Birmingham, but by March 1866, they were back in Sheffield, where their daughter Annie Flewitt Waterfall was born, followed a year later, by daughter Minnie Waterfall.

Henry and his brother Robert must have had further dealings in Birmingham, as Robert, aged 23, was also married in Edgbaston on 26th December 1867. His bride was Eliza Woodhouse, aged 16, whose parents lived at the Hammer and Pincers public house, on Ringinglow Road, Sheffield, where her father David was the innkeeper and a local farmer.

Henry Waterfall seems to have had an interest in politics, like his father James. In October 1868, there were a couple of articles in the Sheffield Daily Telegraph concerning the candidature of Messrs Roebuck and Hadfield for the Nether Hallam Ward in Sheffield.

The first article reported on a crowded meeting that was held at the Upperthorpe Hotel and various speakers voiced their opinions on the candidates. Henry Waterfall *"spoke of Mr. Roebuck's efforts to give the working men of England national education when that question was unpopular."* Henry's uncle John Waterfall also spoke in favour of Mr. Roebuck.

The second article, a few weeks later, reported on another *"numerous and enthusiastic meeting"* at the Howard Hill Hotel. One of the speakers pointed out that Mr. Roebuck intended to pursue a course with respect to trades unions, a course *"which every*

honest and consistent statesman should follow.
Trades unions ought not to be allowed to limit the
number of apprentices in any trade, for such a course
would tend to place apprentices out of the trades of
their choice and into trades for which they might have
no liking. This would produce unskilled labour, and in
many cases, idle and dissolute workmen. Mr. Henry
Waterfall pointed out the selfish legislation of the old
landed interest, and afterwards of the commercial
interest of the middle classes, and expressed a hope
that the working classes would set a better example
by not listening to any party legislation, but give their
votes with a fair consideration to the interests of all
classes and for the welfare and happiness of the
people of England."

Like his father James, who may have been a
supporter of Chartism, Henry Waterfall had Socialist
beliefs and ideas. He continued to be involved in
political matters and in November 1870, a letter
appeared in the Sheffield Daily Telegraph reporting
on a meeting of the burgesses of Upper Hallam in the
schoolroom at Ranmoor. Henry Waterfall was
elected chairman and expressed his support for a Mr
Gatley to be a person qualified to represent the
burgesses of Upper Hallam in the Town Council.

In April 1871, Henry Waterfall, aged 33, was the
manager of a file manufactory, living at 8 Spring Vale,
with his wife Betsy Rose, aged 31, and daughters
Annie and Minnie aged 5 and 4.

They were financially secure enough to have a

domestic servant, Harriet Walton, aged 13, living with them.

Henry's brother Robert, his wife Eliza and their 2 children, Louisa aged 2, and James aged 2 months, were living nearby at Ran Moor.

In July 1871, another daughter, Beatrice, was born to Henry and Betsy Rose. Sadly, Beatrice died at 8 Spring Vale, aged 8 months. The cause of death was stated to be scrofula from birth convulsions, a form of tuberculosis.

Various forms of tuberculosis were to be the cause of several deaths in the family. At that time there was no known cure - the bacillus causing tuberculosis was not identified until 1882 by the German physician Robert Koch. He received the Nobel Prize in physiology or medicine in 1905 for this discovery.

However, Koch did not believe the bovine and human tuberculosis diseases were similar, which delayed the recognition of infected milk as a source of infection. Later, the risk of transmission from this source was dramatically reduced by the invention of the pasteurization process.

Albert Calmette and Camille Guérin achieved the first genuine success in immunization against tuberculosis in 1906. It was called bacillus of Calmette and Guérin (BCG). The BCG vaccine was first used on humans in 1921 in France, but only received widespread acceptance in the USA, Great Britain, and Germany after World War II.

Two and a half years after the death of her daughter, Betsy gave birth to a son, Richard Miles Waterfall, at 8 Spring Vale on 25th January 1874. Richard was to be immortalised in Henry's poem, "My Own Beloved Boy".

Henry continued to be involved in matters of local politics and, in March 1874, attended a dinner held at the Salutation Inn, St Philips Road, which was reported by the Sheffield Daily Telegraph.

This gathering, by forty gentlemen of all parties in the past Parliamentary election, dined together "to manifest their feelings that differences of political opinions should never interrupt friendly relationships." Henry Waterfall proposed a toast to "The Borough Members" stating that "although he did not wish to say anything that might excite political warmth, he could not forego expressing his political opinions which were Conservative, and that he was glad Mr. Roebuck had been returned to Parliament, because that gentleman would be likely to oppose those untimely changes which some people desired to make in our constitution, and which would be merely changes producing no benefit to the country. He then said he wished but to live in the full enjoyment of liberty, and he cared not who governed if that Government did but give that liberty to all, and secure in our foreign relations that liberty for us among other nations, so that the British people might enjoy the full fruits of their talents at home and in all parts of the world. After these remarks, he said that both members were gentlemen far above the common-

place type of men. Mr. Mundella was a man whose character and capacities were of the first rank, and he was glad such men as he were in Parliament. The toast was enthusiastically received."

[John Arthur Roebuck (1801 – 1879) was returned for Sheffield unopposed in May 1849. He was re-elected at Sheffield after a contest in 1852 and 1857, and without opposition in 1859. He headed the poll there in 1865. When civil war raged in the United States of America he violently championed the slave-holders of the South, boasting that Lord Palmerston had cynically confessed to him that he was on the same side. This apparently illiberal attitude led to Roebuck's rejection by Sheffield at the election of 1868, when the liberals returned Mr. Mundella in his stead. His friends gave him £3,000 by way of testimonial. He regained the seat in 1874.

Anthony John Mundella PC (28 March 1825 – 21 July 1897), known as A. J. Mundella, was an English manufacturer, reformer and Liberal Party politician who sat in the House of Commons from 1868 to 1897. He served under William Ewart Gladstone as President of the Board of Trade in 1886 and from 1892 to 1894. Mundella was elected as Member of Parliament for Sheffield in the 1868 general election, after being asked to stand by trade unionist William Dronfield, to defend the interests of labour in the wake of the Sheffield Outrages. The Sheffield Outrages were a series of explosions and murders by a small group of trade unionist militants carried out in Sheffield in the 1860s.]

In 1875, John Ruskin, the Victorian art critic, entered Henry's life. After coming to Sheffield to visit a former student of his, he was taken by the surroundings and saw the opportunity to set up a museum that would meet the needs of the local workers.

He bought a property at Bell Hagg Road, Walkley and installed his former student, Henry Swan, as museum curator. Ruskin had always had a fascination with chivalry and he associated dragon-slaying with social injustice, hence the chosen name – St George's Museum.

Ruskin saw Walkley as particularly suitable, within walking distance of Sheffield's industrial heart but retaining a relationship with the countryside. The property overlooked the Rivelin Valley, an area that Henry held dear.

He insisted that this was 'the only way of permanently bettering the material condition of the poor'.

Metal workers in the city were invited to ascend to the upper reaches of Walkley, where, in addition to the fresh air and the pastoral beauty of the Loxley and Rivelin Valley, they would have sight of various art treasures, including medieval manuscripts, paintings and architecture.

It is not known when and for how long Henry was involved with John Ruskin, but with his love of the Rivelin Valley and his socialist beliefs, the two must have been ideally suited.

By 1876, Henry and his brother Robert were in business together at 24 Bailey Lane, off West Street, Sheffield. Their entry in White's Directory reads *"Manufacturers of Best Refined Cast Steel. Specially adapted for Tools, Chisels, Taps and Dies, Drills, Sates, Cups and Snaps, Hammers, Masons Tools, Cornish Borers etc."*

Just when everything seemed to be going well for the brothers, tragedy struck!

On 8th December 1876, Robert died, at the age of 32, from kidney disease, leaving his wife Eliza, aged 25, with 3 young children. Probate was granted to his widow Eliza and his effects were under £450, about £50,000 in today's money.

Henry must have been distraught, but more unhappiness was to follow. Nine months after Robert's death, on 18th September 1877, his father James, aged 64, passed away, and was buried with Robert at Christ Church, Fulwood.

Probate was granted in October 1878, the executors being Henry Waterfall, file manufacturer, of Steel Bank, and Thomas Hodder Heard, traveller, of Ran Moor. The estate was under £200, about £20,000 in today's money.

Stories passed down through the family indicate that Henry and Robert liked to drink and gamble, and after the deaths of his brother and father, Henry sank even lower.

It seems that Henry tried to mend his ways and regretted his past behaviour. He had always loved poetry – both reading and writing from an early age and in 1880, his book of poetry "Rivelin Rhymes" was published. It was dedicated to the Rev Alfred Gatty, Vicar of Ecclesfield.

The preface to the book of poems gives some indication of the pain and heartache he felt, and his remorse for the things he had done. Unfortunately, Henry did not ultimately succeed in turning away from his "worldly pleasures."

"I have gone after worldly pleasures, even when I have been conscious that I was departing from those virtues of pure, simple, and industrious life on which happiness depends. And that I might be at ease in the pursuit of these pleasures, I have sought them in common with inferior grades of men, and where it was not likely I should meet with reproof. I have slighted the opportunities I have had of promoting my social standing and spiritual welfare. I am soiled in the field of earth, and He whom I honour is far from me, and His face is turned the other way. Yet with none need this be so to the end of life; for although the past must forever remain as we have left it, we may yet, in the days we have to come, merit the material blessings of well-spent time; and in our leisure hours and at home we may enjoy the charms of poetry (to which stock, O may I add a little!) and in the hour of death we may have the consolations of religion.

The composing of these rhymes has been a benefit to myself; it has led me to read more diligently our best authors; made me better acquainted with our language, and above all, convinced me that virtue and piety give the best charms to poetry, and the most lasting enjoyments to life."

The subjects of many of Henry's poems concerned nature, flowers, birds etc. but some were personal, relating to his family. This extract from one of his poems – *My Beloved Boy* - relates to his father James and his son Richard.

My father took me there;
   For he his boyhood spent
In Rivelin valley, and
   Instinctively we went

There, soon as I could walk,
   Our leisure to enjoy;
As I go now with thee,
   My own belovèd boy!

Henry would also submit poetry to the Sheffield Daily Telegraph to pay tribute to local dignitaries who had passed away.

One that was published was for Henry Wilson a snuff manufacturer who set up his company at Westbrook Mill, later selling the business to Imperial Tobacco. Wilsons of Sheffield founded in 1737 was the oldest snuff manufacturing company in the world. It remained in family ownership until 1953, when its elderly proprietors sold the business to Imperial Tobacco. Henry Wilson died on 16th November 1880.

Another was for Mark Firth (of Firth Brown fame), who died 12 days after Henry Wilson. Henry Wilson and Thomas Moore were also mentioned in the poem.

LINES ON THE DEATH OF MARK FIRTH ESQ.

And thou, too, art no more, great-hearted Firth!
And with good Wilson, Moore – thy worthy peers –
Art fall'n in one short autumn to the earth!
The saddest autumn we have had for years.

Pale Hallamshire drew lately round her breast
Her fur robes close, and in the star-lit morn,
When thaw-winds roused the oak woods from their rest,
She sought thy palace gates in grief; there borne

To see if lights were burning still with thee-
And cannot help but seek those gates again,
Dark as dark-windowed Oakbrook House may be,
Amid its dirge-toned trees in wind and rain.
Dec. 1st, 1880   HENRY WATERFALL

Mark Firth was born in Sheffield in 1819. He and his brother set up their own business in 1842. The firm started slowly but by 1852, business was so good that they had to move to larger premises at the Norfolk Works, in Savile Street. The works had crucible furnaces, a file making shop and the largest rolling mill in Sheffield, by 1875 employing over a thousand workers.

Mark Firth became one of the wealthiest people in Sheffield, and in 1875, bought a thirty-six-acre estate which he presented to the town of Sheffield as Firth Park and built a mansion for himself at Oakbrook, Ranmoor on the outskirts of the town. Oakbrook is mentioned in Henry's poem and is now the Notre Dame High School.

On the 16th November 1880, Mark Firth suffered a stroke whilst at the Norfolk Works. He was taken to his home at Oakbrook, but he did not recover. He died on the 28th November 1880 and was buried in the General Cemetery.

Thomas Moore was the owner of the Exchange Brewery and was Mayor of Sheffield for 4 years, and also died in 1880.

By April 1881, Henry and his family had moved to 189 Spring Vale Road in the Crookes area of Sheffield. Henry was now aged 43, and still a steel manufacturer, living with wife Betsy Rose, daughters Annie aged 15, and Minnie aged 14, and son Richard Miles aged 7.

Sometime between 1876 and May 1881, Henry took Edwin Barber into partnership.

The Trade Marks were "Magic" with the symbol of a flying witch, "Prometheus", and "Niagara".

However, on 7th May 1881, probably due to Henry's drinking lifestyle and his declining fortunes, the partnership with Edwin Barber was dissolved by mutual consent, with Edwin Barber accepting all debts due and owing to the firm, which was allowed to continue with the name of the Company i.e. H & R Waterfall and Barber. The Company name remained unchanged until 1976 when it became Hillcliff Tools Limited.

It is likely that Henry Waterfall's alcoholism was to

blame for the family's fall from grace. In 1891, Henry, Betsy and son Richard were now living at 33 Mushroom Lane, a three-storey stone house, which is described by Weston Park Museum as "working class housing". On the census form, Henry, now 53, is described as a commercial traveller in the steel trade. Perhaps he had been employed by one of his many relatives in the trade.   Richard, aged 17, was a file cutter. Also resident on the night of the census was a visitor - Annie Elizabeth Bramhall.

Richard and Annie were both 17 years old and the fact that Annie had stayed overnight at the Waterfall home indicates that they had known each other for a while. Annie lived with her parents, John and Martha Bramhall, at 10 Court, 4 House, Morpeth Street, which was near to Mushroom Lane. It is therefore possible that Richard and Annie either met in the neighbourhood or at their place of work, as they were both file cutters.

Annie became pregnant and, on 14th March 1893, gave birth to Richard's daughter Florence at the Morpeth Street house. They did not, however, get married until 18 months later, and Florence had the surname Bramhall.

Richard's mother Betsy died on 11th November 1893. Betsy must have had a terrible struggle to cope with the change in her circumstances due to Henry's alcoholism, especially since her father and brothers had been successful businessmen in Birmingham.

One of Henry's poems – "Wild Flowers" has a very poignant verse, considering his and Betsy's situation: -

> *Like the children*
> *Of a drunken father, that are*
> *Poor, sweet, and kindly spoken;*
> *So long as grief has not*
> *Their mother's spirit broken.*

The Bramhalls - On early records, the family surname is spelt as Bramall, changing to Bramhall around the 1870s. Not an unusual situation, considering that most of the early Bramalls could not sign their own name, and most of their marriage certificates are signed with an X.

George Bramall was born in the parish of Bradfield in 1794, and in 1821, at the age of 27, married Hannah Fearn, aged 21, the daughter of John and Sarah Fearn. George was a file smith, as were many others in the Bradfield area. George and Hannah had 8 children, their eldest son John, also a filesmith, married Ann Glossop, the daughter of Samuel and Elizabeth Glossop and left the household in 1849.

Although John and Ann, who was pregnant at the time of their marriage in 1849, lived in Portmahon when they married – an area near St Philips Road, Sheffield - they were back in Oughtibridge when their first child Martha Ann was born in September the same year.

In 1851, John aged 25, a file smith, Ann aged 21 and Martha aged 1 were still living in Oughtibridge, at the side of the "Sign of the Cock" public house. Further children were born - John in 1852, Henry in 1854, George in 1857, and Elizabeth in 1858.

Sadly, Ann, aged only 28, died five weeks after giving birth to Elizabeth. The cause of death was puerperal peritonitis, also known as childbed fever. This was not uncommon at that time and was usually caused by a lack of hygiene by doctors and midwives at the time of delivery.

In 1861, John Bramall, aged 35 and now a widower following the death of his wife Ann, was still living near to the "Cock Inn" (formerly the Sign of the Cock) at Oughtibridge and still working as a file smith. He had four of his children with him, Martha aged 11, John aged 9, Henry aged 7, and George aged 4. His youngest daughter Elizabeth, aged 3, was living with John's parents, George, aged 67, and Hannah, aged 62, at New Street, Gate. George was still working as a file smith, as were his sons William and Joseph who were also still resident.

John died in March 1870 aged 44. The cause of death was disease of the heart and lungs, and congestion of the brain. Many filesmiths and file cutters died at an early age due to working in dusty conditions and also from lead poisoning which was used extensively in the workshops. The files were laid on a bed of lead while being worked, and the

men would eat their dinners while sitting at their
benches without first washing their hands.

The File Cutter

He thought he would make a good living,
His family had always been poor,
He uprooted his family by moving
To Sheffield, over the moor.

He found somewhere to live quite quickly,
A two-up two-down in a yard,
Where there were all little workshops for men,
women and kids
With a stool and a bench – it was hard!

He collected the blanks in a barrow,
From somewhere a few miles away,
Then trundled them back to be worked on
For upwards of twelve hours a day.

He sat with his hammer and chisel
And a trench that was filled with lead.
He breathed in the dust and got mucky
But knew that his family was fed.

It was only the bosses who prospered,
He always worked hard and with hope,
With a few short spells in the workhouse,
When his lungs could no longer cope.

The poisonous lead finally killed him,
The family continued to strive
As file cutters all, in the workshop,

And dreamed of a much better life.

In April 1871, John (Junior) was an apprentice file cutter living at Hill Top in the Ellison household. He married Martha Hirst in March 1873.

Martha was pregnant at the time and by the time their daughter Ann Elizabeth was born on 6th July 1873, they were living at Hill Top, Bradfield.

Two more children were born in Oughtibridge - Ada Annie in 1876 and Eliza in 1878 but by the time Clara was born in March 1881, the family were living in Sheffield at 1 Court, 10 Apple Street in the Neepsend area of Sheffield. The family now consisted of Annie, aged 7, Ada aged 4, Eliza, aged 3, and baby Clara. John was still a file cutter.

Eliza died aged 4 in July 1882, and Clara died a few weeks later, aged 18 months. The infant mortality rate in those days was very high especially in industrial areas like Sheffield. In 1882, the family had moved to 10 Court, 5 Wentworth Street and more children followed - Frederick in 1884, John in 1886, and Alice in 1893.

By 1891, Annie Bramhall (John's eldest daughter) had met her future husband Richard Miles Waterfall and had a daughter Florence in March 1893.

It was not until 8th October 1894 that Richard Miles Waterfall and Annie Bramhall were able to marry at St Stephens Parish Church, Sheffield. Richard was still a file cutter, and at the time of their marriage, lived at 63 Crookesmoor Road. Annie lived at 69 Crookesmoor Road with her parents.

After their marriage, it is possible that Richard Waterfall, with his wife Annie and daughter Florence lived with his father Henry. Henry died on 22nd January 1896, aged 58, in the Union Workhouse/Infirmary, suffering hallucinations due to his alcoholism and reciting Walter Scott's "The Lady of the Lake". In Henry's book of poetry – Rivelin Rhymes – the poem "The Birdcatcher" has a few lines that could be applied to Henry's wish to be forgiven for his past: -

When the days of sad bondage are o'er,
And his soul and his birds are set free,
They'll forgive him and whistle in Paradise,
I hope, both for him and for me.

He was buried in Christ Church Fulwood on 27th January 1896. There is no headstone on his grave, unlike the quite impressive headstones on the many other Waterfall graves at Christ Church, but he is buried (with his wife Betsy) near to the grave of his father James, mother Sarah and brother Robert.

For Henry there is merely a flat stone slab with the initials "H.W" in one corner.

So, Richard Waterfall, by the age of 22, had suffered the loss of both his parents. In 1897, a son was born to Richard and Annie, named Henry after his grandfather, followed by a daughter Rose in 1900.

Florence's brothers and sisters all had the surname Waterfall, but Florence, having been born before her parents' marriage, had the surname Bramhall.

By 1901, Richard and Annie, along with their 3 children, Florence, aged 7, Henry aged 3, and Rose aged 1, had moved in with Annie's parents John and Martha Bramhall, who lived with their children John Jnr, aged 15, and Alice, aged 8, at 26 Eden Street, off Driffield Street, between Penistone Road and the River Don.

John, Snr, and son-in-law Richard were file cutters while John Jnr, was a wire cutter.

There were now 10 people in the household, including Martha's mother Hannah, aged 77, who had joined the family after her husband Samuel's death in 1895.

26 Eden Street was terraced housing and the family must have struggled to keep fit and healthy. In the space of 3 years between 1901 and 1904, three more children were born to Richard and Annie but none of these children survived for longer than 4 months. The cause of death for these children was either whooping cough or bronchitis. Frederick lived from June to September 1901, Richard lived from May to September 1903, by which time the family were living at 9Ct 13 House Penistone Road, and Charles was born in July 1904 but died in October the same year. So Florence, at the age of 8 years old, witnessed the births and deaths of 3 baby brothers.

Martha's mother Hannah also died, aged 80, in September 1903, of a cerebral haemorrhage while the family were living at Ct 9 Penistone Road.

In June 1905 and again in August 1905, John Bramhall (Snr) had spells in the workhouse, which was also used as a hospital. John suffered severely from chest problems and was not able to carry on working and contribute to the family income.

Another son, William, was born to Richard and Annie on 2nd March 1907 at number 12 in Court 9, Penistone Road, Ecclesall, Sheffield. This time, the baby survived. Their older children were Florence aged 14, Henry aged 10, and Rose aged 7.

In 1910, Richard and Annie moved to 4 Penistone Road, with their children Florence, Henry, Rose and William. Shortly afterwards, Annie's father John died at the age of 58 from a cerebral haemorrhage.

In April 1911, with both her parents working as file cutters, Florence, aged 18, took over responsibility for looking after the younger children, aged 13, 11 and 4, and keeping house. There were therefore 6 people in the house, which is described on the census form as only having 3 rooms, including the kitchen.

The family then moved to 4 Court, Artisan Street and Florence, by now a machine file cutter, became pregnant and gave birth, aged 19, to her first illegitimate daughter Betsy on 21st April 1912. No father's name was given on the child's birth certificate.

Since Florence's three brothers had all died before reaching the age of 5 months, it was obvious that the family were living in extreme poverty. The cause of death for these babies was usually whooping cough or bronchitis, and tuberculosis was also a common cause of mortality.

Martha Bramhall died on 2nd April 1913 in the workhouse infirmary. The cause of death was spinal caries - a form of tuberculosis.

In early 1914, Richard and Annie had another baby, a daughter Minnie (named after Richard's sister) who sadly only lived for 4 weeks.

By 1916, the family had moved to 23 Percy Street which was to remain the family home for 50 years until Florence (still unmarried and by now a pensioner) was obliged to move to a council flat at 9 Earldom Drive because Percy Street was due to be demolished.

Florence Bramhall aged about 19

William became the youngest surviving child of Richard and Annie. He was a lovable rogue who was the source of much laughter in the family, but he detested school and played truant at every available opportunity. Although he learned to read and write, he never applied himself to serious study. He did, however, do well in his life, spending some time in the army during the war and later having his own greengrocery business.

By the time William was 9 years old, he was attending (or supposed to be attending) Woodside

School on Rutland Road. Whenever he played truant, he would head out of the dirt and grime of his surroundings and into the area of the Rivelin Dams or Wadsley Bridge, which was all countryside at that time.

His father Richard knew of his truancy and warned him time and time again that he would land himself in trouble, but William took no notice. Then one day, the inevitable happened. A policeman (the school bobby) came to the house and sternly told William that he had to pack his case and come along with him.

The whole family were distraught and in tears; even William was sobbing his heart out. His mother tried to console him, saying, "Don't worry. It won't be for long, but you've got to go." They packed him a few clothes in a tiny little attaché case that they had had to borrow from one of the neighbours, and then made their tearful farewells.

He was taken to a place called Hollow Meadows, which was an Industrial School for truants on the outskirts of Sheffield, near to the rolling hills of the Peak District and established by the efforts of Isaac Ironside. As well as receiving some education, the boys were put to work on a farm, working outside in the fields and with animals. After living amongst the smoky streets of the big city of Sheffield, William absolutely loved his time there and was reluctant to return home. When he did return, he did not stop talking about his experiences, telling everyone how much he had enjoyed his punishment, out in the countryside all the time and working in the fields.

Florence, now a domestic servant, had another illegitimate daughter Rose, born at 23 Percy Street in October 1916, but she died at home, at the age of 17 months, of whooping cough and bronchitis.

Florence's eldest daughter, Betsy, was always known by family and friends as "our Bette". When Bette was young, she had an abscess on her face, which needed to be operated on and removed, leaving a small scar. This meant that her mouth was pulled slightly to the side when she smiled but she was still a beautiful young lady.

When William was about 11 years old, he recruited Bette into playing truant with him. She was only 6 years old. He and Bette, after deciding to play truant for the day, would usually go fishing to Rivelin Dams. Knowing that they would be gone all day with nothing to eat, William had a foolproof way of making sure that they would not go hungry. His mother had a "strap shop" which meant that the children were often sent for provisions and the shopkeeper would be paid at the end of the week. William would lay on the tramlines at the bottom of Percy Street, which curved in the direction of Harvest Lane. He would then shout to Bette that he intended to remain lying there until she fetched a cob and some corned beef from the "strap shop".

Bette was terrified that William was going to be run over and killed and begged him to get up, promising that she would go and get the corned beef cob. This ploy worked on numerous occasions, William always managing to get up well before the tram arrived. Years later, William admitted that, with his ear pressed to the tramline, he could hear the vibrations caused by the tram well before it came into view, so was never in any danger of being run over by the tram.

He continued to play truant from school in the fervent hope that the school bobby would come for him again and take him to Hollow Meadows. Unsurprisingly, this did indeed happen, but this time there were no tears; William was sitting on the stairs, waiting for the bobby, with his case already packed! However, this was to be his last time at Hollow Meadows, as he was soon due to leave school and start work.

Richard, Annie and Florence all worked as file cutters. The file cutter's life was not an easy one. The men worked in workshops or factories, seated at a bench with the blank file placed in a bed of lead, so as not to damage the file while the hammer and chisel were used. The weight of the hammer used could be as much as eight or nine pounds. As the work progressed, the lead was turned into a black powder which the file cutter breathed in and which also covered his hands. Many of the file cutters were poisoned by the lead, suffering from severe abdominal pains, vomiting, constipation and epilepsy.

Their teeth and gums were often tinged blue, a common indication of lead poisoning.

Women in the home, whilst cooking and caring for the children also worked as file cutters. Smaller files were cut by the women, using lighter hammers and younger children were also put to work. "Blanks" were collected weekly from a factory and then taken back, sometimes on the bus, and carefully rolled in sacking, so that they did not get damaged before going through the process of hardening.

Although Richard, Annie and Florence all worked as file cutters, Richard's passion was fishing in the Rivelin Valley with his friend "Owd Barrett", who was always the subject of an amusing story or incident. It was always "Owd Barrett" who was the object of the joke, or who had done something silly, or embarrassing - never Richard!!

Richard started to make fishing rods to supplement the family income and soon became a skilled craftsman. People came from miles around to buy them and he also supplied many members of the All-England teams. The fishing rods were so well made, they would last a lifetime.

Times continued to be hard, however.

Richard and Annie's youngest child William left school in about 1920. As his favourite part of his stay at Hollow Meadows truant school was working with the horses, he went to work for a deliveryman who had horses and carts. William was not allowed to drive the horses at first and worked alongside an older man, but as he got older and more experienced, he was permitted to drive his own horse and cart. As stated, he loved horses but, ironically, it was to be a shire horse that knocked down and trampled his 18-month-old daughter Thelma to death when he was 26 years old.

Richard and Annie's eldest child Florence had another illegitimate daughter in January 1920, whom she named Ada, after her mother's sister. Ada survived childhood.

Their son Henry had married Lilian Walton in 1919. Henry and Lilian lived at 23 Percy Street for a while and their daughter Minnie was born in November 1920 but sadly was another childhood casualty and died by February 1921, aged 3 months. Another daughter Lilian, born in 1922, survived.

Their daughter Rose married Fred Wilkinson on 26th April 1921 and they too were living at 23 Percy Street when daughter Elizabeth was born a couple of weeks later. Sadly, Elizabeth only lived for 14 days. Another child Fred born in May 1922 survived, and Rose and Fred moved to their own home at 19 Percy Street.

Child mortality was extremely high in the family – no doubt caused by living conditions at that time. The family must have been extremely poor, and the situation was not improved by the fact that in September 1925, Florence had another illegitimate daughter, also named Florence, who was born in the Children's Home attached to Fir Vale Workhouse on Smilter Lane.

When William left school, Bette continued playing truant on occasions and when her younger sister Ada started school at age 5, Bette initiated her into also playing truant. Bette would be 12 years old at this time. Mrs Reynolds, a neighbour, who lived in the same yard at Percy Street was asked to take Bette and Ada to school along with her own daughter Mary.

There were three arches on Rutland Road, the big one in the middle for the traffic to go through, and a little one on either side for pedestrians. Woodside school was at the top of the hill. Mrs Reynolds was persuaded by Bette to leave them at the three arches, to avoid having to climb the hill, promising her that they would continue the rest of the way to school by themselves.

The children watched Mrs Reynolds from the arches and, as soon as they saw her go around the top of Percy Street, they would run down Rutland Road to freedom. Sometimes it was pouring with rain, but that did not dampen their enthusiasm to play truant. They rarely had money for bus fares, but sometimes had a halfpenny in their pocket. They would make their way to a little playground nearby, where an old chap had a few swing-boats. They would sit there in the pouring rain, swinging away to their hearts' content, while the boat steadily filled with water. The old chap would let them stay on indefinitely provided no other customers were waiting.

Sometimes, if they had a penny or two, they would go to Wadsley Bridge on the tram or to Rivelin Dams and just wander about all day. It was a real adventure for them, going into what they thought of as "the countryside". Bette was never sent away for truancy, unlike her uncle William.

When Bette was 14, in 1926, the family were in dire straits, possibly because Florence, her mother, had had a baby in September the previous year, and was unable to work. Richard and Annie were also struggling to survive, so Bette and Ada had to be admitted into Fir Vale Workhouse.

Bette was immediately put to work in the kitchen and Ada, who was only 6 years old, was told to go and play in the yard. Ada, feeling very lonely and abandoned, kept running to look through the kitchen window to make sure that Bette was still there, only to be told by Bette to go and play, as she was busy. They did share a bedroom, however, but it was like a little prison cell, with a window so high that they could only see the sky, nothing else.

One day, Bette shouted, "Mi Granddad's here!" and Ada, excited and jumping up and down, responded with "Where? Where?" Their beloved granddad, Richard Waterfall, was sitting on a bench in the passageway, waiting for them. Richard had already asked the staff to fetch their things, he was now able to take his grand-daughters home.

A large oval tin was produced which had been used to store Ada's crepe soled sandals. The children had been issued with clogs on their arrival. Unfortunately, the tin had been placed somewhere warm and the crepe soles had curled up with the heat, making them impossible to wear and had to be thrown away.

Since the clogs had only been loaned to the children, they had to be returned to be used by the next lot of children, so Richard had to carry Ada all the way home on his shoulders.

Florence's new baby daughter Florence only managed to survive one year and died in October 1926 of pneumonia.

The family continued to struggle for survival, more so after Florence gave birth to another illegitimate daughter Alice in 1928.

None of the 5 daughters that had been born to Florence were registered with a father's name on the birth certificate and it was never established who fathered these babies. Ada later admitted that she had never questioned her mother about her father's identity, as "it was not something you talked about in those days." Throughout her life Ada wondered who her father was. Having 5 children out of wedlock was so out of character for Florence who was always very straight-laced with very high standards.

Florence never married, and it was likely that all the children had the same father. When the youngest daughter Alice was a baby, Ada remembered a strange conversation between the adults, with someone saying, "it's about time he faced up to his responsibilities," but Ada was not quite sure who they were talking about and was too afraid to ask. She was never aware of any man on the scene who could have been her father.

Another strong memory from Ada's early childhood was of her Uncle Fred, who was married to her mother's sister Rose and was a bit of a tease, telling her that it was such a shame that her father had died in the war. Ada believed this to be true, and it was not until she was a few years older that Ada realised that since the war had ended in 1918, it could not possibly have been true as she was born in 1920.

The family did make good use of Annie's skills in providing enough food to feed the family. A ham shank would be bought for sixpence from a butcher's on Shalesmoor. It would be boiled in a great big pan with split peas and lentils. Henry's wife Lilian would chop up all the vegetables - carrots, turnips, celery, onions and finally a bag of pot herbs would be thrown in. On the first day, the family would only eat the vegetables and the stock, not the meat, saving the ham shank for the next day, when it would be served up with mashed potatoes and any other vegetables they had left.

Another day, they would have fish, but never fillets of fish. Annie would buy fish pieces – as much as she could afford - and bake them in a big square tin, ending up with a sort of thick mushy fish sauce. It would then be dished up with a big serving of mashed potatoes and peas, with freshly baked bread to mop up the "fish".

Another meal would be corned beef hash, again stewed with plenty of vegetables. The corned beef cost tuppence halfpenny for half a pound.

Annie would also make use of the fact that if you went to the market late on Saturday afternoon, you might be able to get a bargain buy of meat or fish, as there were no freezers in those days. After queuing with many others with the same thought in mind, she would return triumphantly with a leg of lamb for sixpence, or, if she had not been successful in the meat queue, with a whole cod from the fishmonger. This would then be served up for Sunday dinner.

The children also used to visit the local pork butcher on Harvest Lane, an old German chap called Funk, who kept and killed his own pigs. He was a lovely friendly old man and the children would take a basin and a bagful of all their peelings from the vegetables for him to feed to his pigs. In return, he would give them a bread cake dipped in pork dripping with a bit of crackling on the top. The basin was for Richard's quarter of roast pork, which was an occasional treat. Mr Funk knew that Richard was not too bothered about the meat, but he did love the crispy bits, so he would fill the basin with all the bits of crispy pork. When these were removed later, there was a decent amount of pork dripping left in the bottom of the basin that was spread on bread, providing another tasty meal for the family. Nothing was wasted. Mr Funk also had pigs' bladders hung up in the shop filled with lard. When these were empty, he would blow them up and tie a knot in them and then give them to the local children to use as footballs. These improvised footballs lasted for ages.

The family continued to struggle to survive and any opportunity was grabbed in order to earn a bit of extra money. Annie took in washing and ironing from Monday morning until Sunday night, which earned half a crown for each load. Bette and William would fetch the washing on Monday morning from one of four houses on Ball Bridge, near Neepsend Lane. The people there all had full time jobs, and their houses were thought to be very "posh", having long curtains as well as nets. One house would have their washing collected on a Monday, another on a Tuesday and so on. It was then washed, dried and taken back after it had been ironed. There was a copper boiler in the corner of the kitchen at Percy Street with a fire underneath, which had to be kept going all the time. Annie would wash all the clothes on her knees with a rubbing board, and the communal yard would be continuously full of other people's washing until it dried. It would then be ironed before sending it back to the customer. It was backbreaking work.

The children also attempted to earn extra money for the family in several ways. Bette and Ada would go to a woodyard on Rutland Road to buy off-cuts, which they fetched home in a barrow. They couldn't afford to use coal every day to heat the water for Annie's washing, so the larger knotted pieces were used to stoke the fire under the copper boiler, and Richard then chopped up the smaller pieces and tied them into bundles. Bette and Ada then went around the streets with the barrow, knocking on doors and selling the firewood. Bette would push the barrow, with little Ada jumping up and down at her side and pestering to be allowed to push it. They were given instructions by Richard to charge a penny a bundle, but if they had trouble selling it, they could reduce the price to a halfpenny.

All monies earned went into the household budget. At that time Richard was only getting about 10 shillings a week (about £20 in today's money) and Annie got a half a crown for each load of washing.

Florence would be provided with her meals when she worked as a domestic servant, but when she started work at Sheffield Infirmary, she would take a breadcake with her for her dinner.

Nearly every family baked their own bread, the smell of it hanging about in the street. The bakers such as Gunstones used to make pastries rather than bread. Little local shops would sell cobs, which were usually made by the shopkeeper on the premises. Annie baked half a stone of bread every other day. She was very often ill, but never took to her bed, fearing that the family would not survive without her contribution to the family income.

After Bette left school at the age of 14, Ada attended school regularly. She was a very bright pupil and enjoyed going to school.

Despite having children, Florence continued to work, firstly as a domestic servant, then at the Infirmary.

On one occasion, Florence was ill and unable to go to work to the private house where she was employed as a domestic servant. The employer turned up at the back door, and Florence was standing at the table, with daughter Ada at the sink, and her father Richard in his armchair. This well-dressed man in a large overcoat started to shout at Florence, stating that he could have her sent to prison for not turning up and for letting them down. Florence started swaying as she stood there terrified, and then fainted on the floor. Ada ran out of the house screaming, thinking her mother had died. When Richard ordered him to leave, he threatened that he would have all of them put away. Richard refused to let Florence return to that employer, and she soon found work at the Royal Infirmary as a cleaner, where she stayed for about 20 years. She worked from 6 a.m. until 6 p.m. for 18 shillings a week.

23 Percy Street was a very small 2 bedroomed property, with an outside toilet, that over the years housed many of the growing Waterfall family as well as the older ones after marriage. The young couples could occupy the downstairs front room until finding a place of their own. The younger children in the family often had to share the bedroom of their grandparents.

Bette was very musical, and the entire local neighbourhood knew about it. From the age of about 12, she had been accustomed to being called from the streets into the local pubs to "give us a tune on the piano, Bette". She would play any tune requested, but only by ear, not being able to read music. Realising her talent, her family managed to buy her an old piano and scraped the money together for her to have piano lessons. Her piano teacher, who lived on Burton Road, was the grandmother of Reginald Dixon, the famous organist who played at the Tower Ballroom in Blackpool from 1930 onwards, becoming known as "Mr Blackpool."

After five or six lessons, her piano teacher, realised that Bette was fighting a losing battle by trying to read music and said, "Look, Bette, I'm taking your money under false pretences. You'll never learn to play by reading music. Continue as you are, playing by ear, and you'll do very well."

Bette's piano was in the front room and the door opened directly onto the street. She loved playing for the local children who would gather round the open front door, requesting different tunes and dancing in the street.

When Bette was 15 she had been hanging about with a group of friends including a lad called Frank Bell, who was a couple of years older than her. He had managed to acquire an old photograph of her, and when he showed it to her, she told him it was a terrible photo and grabbed it from him and ripped it up and threw it down at his feet. Shortly after, he joined the army and was posted to India. She received a few letters from him initially, but soon forgot all about him.

This photo dated 1929 shows Bette at the age of 16 or 17.

Although there was not much spare money about for toys, the children were very good at improvising. In the Woodside area, near to Wigfall's, was a factory that made all sorts of plastic items, mainly combs. The children used to go to the waste dumped at the back of the building and pick out bits of broken combs of all shapes, sizes and colours.

They also visited the rear of the tobacconist and sweet shops, to collect all the dummy boxes of chocolates and cigarettes that had been used in window displays. These, along with the broken combs, were used to play at shop in the communal yard of the houses. Annie would tolerate the mess that the children made, with the warning "You'd better clear all those up when you've finished." The children stored their "shop" in the yard, or even in the outside toilets, until the boxes were torn and unusable. They would then be cleared away and put into the dustbin.

The outside toilets were grim places, poorly lit and situated across the yard from the houses. Ada was frightened to go to visit the toilet in the dark, so when she had to go, she would run across the yard, singing her heart out and continue singing until she got back to the safety of the house! Her reasoning for this was that if she stopped singing because something or someone had grabbed her, the family would know immediately and come looking for her.

Another game played by the children was the peg top. This was a small wooden top with a nail at the bottom. String was wrapped round it with the end of the string in the palm of the hand. It was then slung onto the floor where it spun for ages. A variation of this game was where a square was drawn on the ground and each child put a halfpenny inside the square. The children then took it in turns to spin the top, pocketing any halfpenny that they managed to knock out of the square. This game was for the older, more adept children. The younger ones had a top with a whip to make it spin.

Battledore and shuttlecock was another popular game. The older children had shuttlecocks with extra-long feathers that were hit as far as possible up into the air, returning to earth with a superb spinning motion. The younger children were told that they were too young to play with these and had to make do with a large bat and a small shuttlecock.

Diabolos were also popular. These were like a large spool that narrowed in the middle. Two sticks joined by a piece of string were used to roll the diabolo from one stick to the other, spinning it all the time. The children practised for hours and competed with each other as to how long they could be kept going and whether they could be thrown up into the air and caught again.

Percy Street was often taken over by whole families for skipping. There was no traffic in those days, and a long rope was stretched from one side of the street to the other. Everyone joined in, even the adults. Sometimes two ropes were used – this was called French skipping.

Another game was "Peggy". A short stick was balanced on a brick. A longer stick was held by the player who then hit the "peggy" at one end to make it fly up in the air before hitting it again. The winner was the person who managed to hit it for the longest distance.

"Chasing round the lump" was also a favourite pastime. One child would run up Percy Street, onto Burton Road, then along Neepsend Lane and back up Percy Street. Another child would set off at the same time but running around in the opposite direction. The first back to the start was declared the winner.

At the back of the house on Percy Street was a factory called Joseph Pickerings where "Blanco" was made. This was like a white chalk that was used to whiten and waterproof leather and other materials. The children would climb over the wall after the workers had gone home and gather any pieces of Blanco that were lying about. These would be used as chalk in various games, such as hopscotch. The pieces of Blanco would be of no use after getting damp from being out in the open, but the children would still be chased off the premises by any men who happened to be working late.

Another place where the children hung about was Neepsend Rolling Mills on Neepsend Lane. They would enter the gates, especially during the wintertime, as it was nice and warm there. The ingots of red-hot steel, being rolled out was a fascinating sight for the children. The workers would shout, "Get your bloody selves away!" The children did not realise that the workmen were all too aware of the danger of them being so close to the rolls that could fall the wrong way. On some occasions, they were threatened with the bobby if they refused to move away from the warmth. If he did appear and chased them off, they would return when he had gone and stand against the wall, which was lovely and warm.

As the houses were all terraced and had communal yards, the children would often run about up and down the passages, over the walls and into adjoining yards. They used to get into terrible trouble for this, often receiving a clip round the ear from the local bobby, an event that was expected and accepted in those days.

One of Ada's daily chores, before she went to school, and at dinnertimes when she came home for her dinner, was to call on one of the neighbours – a Mrs Smith who lived at number 27 – to see if she wanted any errands running or any jobs doing. Ada, at the tender age of seven, had inherited this task from her sister Bette who had now left school and started work.

Mrs Smith had an unmarried daughter who had a little boy called Philip. Philip had been conceived when the daughter worked at one of the big houses in Fulwood. Philip's father used to come now and again to see the child and pay something towards his support, but this man was always known as "uncle" and the daughter was not allowed to go back to work for the family.

Florence, on the other hand, received no support for any of her daughters.

Mrs Smith had married daughters, but she still had a husband and several sons living at home, which was a little two-up two-down, the same as all the others on the street. Ada used to wonder where everyone in the Smith family slept as there were so many of them. All the men of the family worked at Neepsend Rolling Mills, so the family was relatively well-off.

Mrs Smith would send Ada to the local shop for some potted meat or corned beef for the sons' sandwiches, even though Mrs Smith's granddaughter Mary Reynolds was usually in the house. Although only 7 years old, Ada was more or less employed by Mrs Smith, who gave Ada threepence a week. Out of this princely sum, Mrs Smith held back one penny to save for Ada "for her holidays."

Sometimes, if there were no errands to run, Ada would be asked to clean the fireplace. She removed all the ashes, and then cleaned the hearth with potmole. This was a ring of a blue and white substance and a piece was broken off and rubbed round the hearth to clean it. If Ada had not cleaned the fire out in the morning before school, she would be expected to do it at dinnertime.

There were no school dinners at that time, so every day Ada returned at lunchtime to Percy Street, but was instructed to call at Mrs Smith's first to do her chores. She would then go home for something to eat, usually a sandwich or liver and onions, made by her Granddad, before going back to school for afternoon lessons.

At teatime she was again expected to call at Mrs Smith's on her way home from school. Mrs Smith would usually be baking bread. With such a large family, she had to make a stone of bread every day. The dough would be taken to a local baker's to be baked. The bakery was along Neepsend Lane, over Ball Bridge towards Shalesmoor, and situated on a little side street. The baker would charge a halfpenny a loaf and Ada would either take it on a barrow to be baked or go and collect it when ready. She liked to watch him load all the loaves onto a big shovel before putting them into the large oven.

Most households made their own bread at that time. An occasional small cob would be bought from the local shop, but not very often. The baker supplied the bread tins and the greaseproof paper that went in them, and he would give his customers a slip of paper to write their name on. He would then tell you a time to come back and collect your order, normally the same day, but if the dough had been taken in towards the end of the day, it would not be ready until the following day. Ada's grandma Annie always did her own baking, either because her family was not as big, or, more likely, to save money which was always tight.

At Christmas-time, fruit cakes and seed cakes would also be taken for baking. At this time of year, Ada had to make two trips with the barrow loaded with everything that Mrs Smith wanted baking for Christmas. Even though Mrs Smith had children and grandchildren, Ada was still expected to do the running about for the Smith family. But one day, Ada had had enough and rebelled!!

She was in the front room and her Granddad was in the kitchen. "Ada, you're wanted," shouted Granddad from the kitchen. Ada thought that Mrs Smith had merely shouted her from the yard and, shouted back, "I'm not going, I've been twice already, and I'm not going again." Granddad repeated, "Ada, you're wanted." Ada flounced through to the kitchen, shouting, "I said I'm not going again!" She was then rooted to the spot by the sight of Mrs Smith's grand-daughter, Mary Reynolds, standing in the kitchen. Ada went beetroot red and fervently wished that the floor would open up beneath her feet. She did not know what to say or do and dreaded the thought of next going into Mrs Smith's, believing that Mary would no doubt have told her what she had said. Mrs Smith, however, never mentioned it to Ada, and did, indeed, take her on holiday – a day trip to the seaside. Ada had never seen the sea before and her first reaction was to exclaim, "Look at all that watter!"

Mrs Smith was also good to the family in other ways. She was a great big woman with rosy cheeks who made sure her husband and working sons were well fed. She would regularly have a great big pan of stew on the go, and, if there was any left, would offer it to Ada's family, saying, "Can you use this up?" They knew that she would always help if needed, and suspected that she had deliberately cooked enough for both families but wanted to preserve the Waterfall family's dignity.

Mrs Smith had a daughter that lived near Grimsby who, every Christmas, used to send a hamper for the Smith family. The daughter was thought to live on a farm because included in the hamper was a great big joint of ham, a turkey and presents for all the family. Ada was usually there at the unpacking, jealously wishing that somebody would send her family something so grand.

Richard and Annie did, however, sometimes receive a small wicker basket in a box from Richard's brother-in-law in Dinnington. Richard would receive a notice from the tramways for him to pick it up at a certain time. The basket was transported on Wigmore's bus from Dinnington to Fitzalan Square and would then be put onto a tram. Richard would wait at the bottom of Percy Street for the tram at the designated time. These deliveries would come at Christmas or sometimes during the year. They usually contained a joint of beef or pork, but mainly second-hand clothes that their family had grown out of. When Ada knew a delivery was due, she would be so excited to discover whether there would be anything in it for her.

Ada's older sister Bette was a good cook and at the age of 18 was employed to cook for the students living in the halls of residence at Collegiate Crescent, Sheffield. This was quite a responsible job for someone as young as 18 and she really enjoyed it. However, at the age of 20, she obtained the post of cook at the Windsor Hotel in Blackpool. She had heard about the job from a neighbour Nellie Senior who lived next door to her in Percy Street. The job was paid slightly better than the job at the college and she would also live in and get her meals. The only disadvantage was that the work was seasonal, lasting from April to October, so money had to be saved to cover the period from November to March, usually from tips earned at the hotel. The other advantage was that Bette's absence from Percy Street would relieve the overcrowding in the house from April to October.

Bette continued to be a favourite of the local children who loved her. Money was not plentiful, but Bette would always be reminded if a child's birthday was imminent. She would take it upon herself to go around all the neighbours begging for "owt to spare?" Nobody had a lot to give, but she would succeed in getting a quarter pound of margarine here, half a jar of jam there, a loaf or two, until she had enough to put together a decent spread. She would then approach the local church and borrow all their crockery and some trestle tables. She would tell them that it was for a child's birthday. Although she could not afford to pay for them, she would promise to look after them, clean them and bring them straight back and the church, knowing her and that nobody had any money to spare, would agree. Bette would then get all the children to help, putting the long trestle tables down the middle of the street and making sure that the birthday child had a day to remember.

When she was away working in Blackpool, the children would always be asking, "When is Bette coming home?" If she was away in Blackpool when a child had a birthday, she would make sure that the child still had a party when she returned. If the child's birthday occurred during the winter months, she would take them out for the day to Endcliffe Woods or Endcliffe Park.

Bette was, however, no softie if she felt that someone was being taken advantage of. In Bette's household, although money was not plentiful, the family were good at managing what little they had, and the rent was the first weekly outgoing to be paid, ensuring that at least the family had a roof over their heads.

In those days, no-one had a bank account, but there existed a savings scheme called a "Diddlum" club. A beginning was made with a halfpenny, then the next week a penny, then three halfpence and so-on. A collector used to come every week and collect it, and savers would draw it out at Christmas or for special occasions.

There was also a "cheque club" where people paid in a weekly amount and then eventually got a "cheque" to spend at various department stores, such as Banners at Attercliffe Common. Florence used to run one of these. The next-door neighbour, Irene, was a customer, but was totally irresponsible when it came to money matters. She would receive her cheque for £10, for which she had paid £11, and then go and buy bedding or other items for the house. Then, because she was short of money, she would sell them to her neighbours for less than she had paid because she needed the ready money. In this way, the neighbours got a better deal than going to the sales. Irene would then have to continue paying the weekly amount to the collector.

This same neighbour, although always short of money, managed to go out at the weekend with her husband but invariably failed to put aside the rent money which was due every Monday. So she would call and borrow the rent from Granddad Richard on a Monday morning, with a promise to pay it back to him on the Friday.

When Bette found out about this arrangement, she tackled Granddad about it, saying "You are daft, Granddad, you're paying two lots of rent." Granddad replied "Nay, she never fails to give it me back on Friday, I'm only helping her out." But Bette could see the fault in Grandad's logic and would not be deterred. "Yes, but you give it her back again every Monday, so it's never your money. I'm going to have a word with her on Friday when she comes around."

When the neighbour appeared on the Friday to repay Granddad, Bette said to her, "Keep that money – put it away and use it to pay your rent on Monday. Don't come borrowing any more money from my Granddad as he can't afford it. You've got your rent now, so don't come borrowing again." The neighbour did not speak to Bette for quite a while after that, but Bette had made her point and knew that she had to protect her good-natured Granddad from being exploited.

She did have a heart of gold, though. When the season finished at Blackpool, although she had saved as much as she could from her wages and tips, she would have to sign on the dole, for which she received about 12 shillings and sixpence. On her way back from the dole office, she would buy some fish or other provisions for the family. But if, on the way, she happened to see a child with no shoes on, she would take him or her into the local Woolworth's to buy a pair of plimsolls, explaining to Granddad on her return why she had only got 5 shillings left to put into the household coffers. She knew that she had always been successful at quickly finding another job.

In July 1931, Richard and Annie's youngest son William married Rose Billard and their daughter Thelma Rose was born in October the same year. The three of them lived at 23 Percy Street. It was common practice at that time, when a couple married, for them to occupy the downstairs front room of their parents' house to use as a bed-sit until they managed to find a home of their own to rent.

The house was only a four-roomed house with an outside toilet and no bathroom; so, one upstairs bedroom was occupied by Richard and Annie, and the other by Florence and her 3 daughters.

When Annie became too ill to work, she taught the girls how to bake the family bread as she lay on the settee. Ada, about 11 years old, would knead the dough in a pancheon on an old kitchen chair that had no back on, and, pummelling away, would ask her grandma "Is it ready yet Grandma?" The answer would always be "No, not yet, get kneading it, it's not ready yet". When Annie was satisfied that it had been kneaded enough, Ada would put the dough to rise before baking it.

When Ada was about 10, there had been a sort of talent competition at school. Pupils were invited to give a performance, either singing, dancing, playing an instrument etc. Ada thought for a long time about what she could possibly do and finally decided to go on stage and whistle! She was very good at imitating various bird songs and also at whistling a tune. To her great joy, she won a prize! Simple achievements like this gave Ada a great deal of pride.

At the age of 11, Ada passed the exam that enabled her to go to Burngreave School. She was so thrilled!

She was supposed to have a full school uniform, but as the family could not afford to completely kit her out, they made sure Ada was clean and tidy and did, in fact, manage to buy her a second-hand blazer. On her first day, she proudly stood in the large hall and waited for her name to be called and to be directed to her nominated classroom. Although she did not know any other children there, she was not worried and was eagerly looking forward to making some new friends.

Ada's joy did not last long. Alice, her younger sister was due to start school. As her mother had no choice but to work to support the family, there was no-one to look after Alice and take her to school. Granddad Richard had to visit the Education Offices to arrange for Ada to be transferred back to Woodside School.

But, as usual, although extremely disappointed, Ada calmly accepted this turn of events. She reminded herself that she could continue to play in the netball and rounders teams, which she loved and excelled at.

The Woodside team used to go to other schools in the Sheffield area and were usually very successful, even when playing against older children, or children who lived in "posh" areas. Ada was particularly fond of one teacher at Woodside School, a Miss Warner.

The families of the children in the school team could not afford to buy sports kits, but Miss Warner managed to provide them with a cream blouse, green tunic and green knickers. They were only allowed to use them when they played against other schools and afterwards, they had to put them back into the boxes along with the tissue paper, taking the knickers home to be washed and returned. The children thought they were marvellous and took very good care of them.

On one occasion Ada was the only one selected out of all the school to go to a running event at Bramhall Lane football ground. She was over the moon and so proud! Ada turned up in her shabby skirt and blouse and her navy-blue knickers. Looking at the other children, in their smart outfits, she felt extremely uncomfortable. To her shame, Ada was eliminated in the first event. She went home as soon as the race was over, not bothering to stay and watch the rest of the races.

Her Granddad was surprised to see her back so soon, and Ada burst into tears, saying, "They were all better than me, I never come anywhere", later admitting to herself that it was not being beaten in the race that had upset her, but the fact that she felt that all the other children were so much better kitted out.

She did, however, have other triumphs that made up for this setback. All the Sheffield schools took part in a netball tournament and she was in the team. After beating Abbeydale School, the team got through to the final, but were then defeated. It was a major achievement for a school such as Woodside to have got so far, and Miss Warner presented every member of the team with a little plaque with their name on. Ada treasured it for years.

On one occasion, Ada, aged 12, and cousin Fred, two years younger, found themselves in trouble with the local bobby. Fred's father, who was married to Ada's aunt Rose, was out of work. This did not happen very often, he was normally employed as a ganger earning 30 shillings a week, in charge of a gang that dug the roads and laid pipes. To make a bit of money, he started to make necklaces and earrings, using gold wire and beads. He instructed Ada and Fred to go around the streets selling them, going from door to door. On their travels, they were spotted and questioned by the local bobby who asked whether they had a license to sell their wares. They did not even know what a license was and explained that Fred's father had made them. The bobby told them, "Well, tell your dad he needs a license." When the children returned home, Fred senior decided it was not worth the hassle to make any more and he found employment soon after.

But one thing Uncle Fred did, was offer to pierce Ada's ears with a darning needle and a piece of cork placed at the back of her ear. The old wives' tale was that it improved your eyesight, and Ada's mother and her aunt Rose had both had theirs done. However, when he pierced one ear, Ada, in pain, screamed and ran out of the house, shouting that there was no way he would be allowed to do the other one. She was eventually persuaded to return indoors to have the other one done. When Ada turned up at school with her pierced ears, the other children started calling her "Gypsy" as it was not usual for girls to have their ears pierced in those days. When she returned home from school, Ada took her earrings out and allowed the holes in her ears to heal, so she had suffered all that pain for nothing.

One day, in early January 1933, Annie was extremely ill and had to be moved from the settee to her bed. She was only 59 years old but to Ada she had always seemed like a very old woman. Ada stood at the bottom of her grandma's bed and it began to dawn on her how seriously ill she was. Her mother and her aunt Rose told her to take the younger children out for an hour or two. When the children returned, Annie had died. She had suffered from chest problems for several years, probably aggravated by her work as a file cutter, and she died of chronic bronchitis and tuberculosis.

She was laid out in the front room downstairs, a normal practice at that time. Ada normally slept in the same bedroom as her mother and sister Bette but was afraid to go to sleep in the bedroom where her grandma had died, knowing that she was lying dead downstairs. She started to cry and was allowed to go to sleep with her beloved Granddad in the next bedroom. Annie was buried in Wardsend cemetery a few days later.

The family could not afford a headstone so son-in-law Fred (married to Rose) acquired a flagstone and spent long hours chiselling an inscription on it. Annie's son William pushed it all the way to the cemetery on a barrow, but, unfortunately, the vicar at the church there would not allow it to be erected. William was adamant that he was not going to push it all the way back again on his barrow, so propped it up at the side of the cemetery gates, where it stood for many years.

After Annie's death, it fell to Florence to manage the house, and care for the family, whilst continuing to work at Sheffield Infirmary that luckily was only a short walk away from Percy Street. At that time Ada and Alice were still at school but were expected to help with household chores every day even doing jobs for some of the neighbours to earn extra money to go into the household coffers.

At the time of Annie's death, son William and daughter-in-law Rose were still resident with their daughter Thelma, aged 15 months.

Thelma

The terraced house on Percy Street was situated, like many in that time, in a communal yard shared by eight houses. There was one passage in the middle of the yard leading to the front of the houses and the street.

William had put a gate at the top of the passage to protect his toddler Thelma, even though there were family and neighbours in the same yard all too ready to keep an eye on her at various times during the day. In April 1933, Rose was doing the weekly wash, coming in and out of the house with her wash basket to peg out the washing in the yard. William shouted to his wife that he was going to the outside toilet. Rose thought that Thelma was still inside the house.

However, unknown to everyone, an insurance man had called to a house in the yard and then left by the passage, leaving the gate open. Thelma went down the passage and onto the street. In those days, there was not that much traffic on Percy Street, but Thelma continued to toddle down the quiet street and on to the busier Burton Road. At that moment a shire horse was passing, pulling a dray - a low heavy cart used for haulage. Thelma toddled under its feet and was trod on by the horse. She died soon afterwards at the Royal Infirmary Sheffield.

An inquest was held and it was found that the cause of death was multiple internal injuries including fractured ribs caused by being knocked down and trod on by a horse drawing a dray. The incident was deemed to be an accident with no post mortem necessary.

The inquest was reported in the local press.

"An accident in Burton Road, Neepsend, Sheffield in which a little girl, 18 months of age, was knocked down and fatally injured by a horse, was described at the inquest held yesterday on Thelma Rose Waterfall of 23 Percy Street, Neepsend, Sheffield.
The mother said her baby was playing in the yard. Shortly after, a neighbour came to tell her that her daughter had been knocked down.
She went to Burton Road where she saw a crowd of people and the child laying on a dray. The baby was taken to the Sheffield Royal Infirmary, where she died on admission.

Joe Warboys, of 28 Percy Street, stated he was in the street, when he saw the little baby crossing Burton Road. She was alone. He noticed a heavy horse dray going along the road towards the city. The child was only about a yard from the horse's head and he shouted to the driver of the dray – who was seated on the edge of the dray, and whose view was obstructed by the horse.

The driver applied his reins, but he was too late. The child was knocked down by the horse's front legs and was trampled on by the hind legs. The wheels of the dray went clear of her body.

He did not think that the driver saw the child at all. Another witness stated that he saw the child "like a bundle of rags under the horse's feet."

Alfred Key, of 10 Clun Road, Pitsmoor, Sheffield, a carter for the LMS Railway, said that when he heard Warboys shouting and noticed him pointing to the horse's feet, he looked down and saw the child between the fore and hind legs of the horse. He pulled on the reins and saw the offside hind leg strike the child in the stomach. Before Warboys shouted, he had not seen the child.

The jury returned a verdict of "Accidental death" and exonerated the driver of the cart from blame." The family was traumatised by the death. Everyone said that the driver must have been asleep - surely to God he could have seen her!

Thelma's father William, who had always loved horses, said that the horse, in common with other animals such as elephants, would have done everything possible so as not to tread on her. He judged that the horse had tried to kick her out of the way, but she must have rolled under its stomach where he could not see her.

Thelma's clothes were brought back from the hospital and shown to the family – the imprint of the horseshoe was plainly visible on her clothes. Everyone sobbed, and her mother Rose declared "there could not possibly be a God to take a babby like that who had never done anything wrong".

There was a lot of talk about "what if?"

Bette was going to the station that day to see about trains to go back to Blackpool to work. She had pleaded with Rose to be allowed to take Thelma with her, but Rose had refused because "she's mucky and needs a bath". Bette had suggested just putting her coat on, but Rose still refused because she was "too mucky". Grandad Richard was going to get some baccy and Thelma wanted to go with him, but again Rose had refused because she was "too mucky."

Ada herself would normally have been home from school and would have played with her and looked after her, but that day she had been playing rounders after school and did not arrive home until after Thelma had been killed.

Thelma was buried in Wardsend Cemetery in the grave of her grandmother Annie Elizabeth Waterfall who had died only 4 months previously.

In those days, there were no counselling services available and the family had to cope alone with their grief. Everyone thought the world of Thelma. The family tried to comfort each other as best they could, but cried for days on end, with her mother Rose close to having a nervous breakdown and declaring that she would never have another child.

Later that year, Bette was away in Blackpool and Ada, as usual, was really missing her big sister. One day, Ada decided to visit her Grandma's grave at Wardsend cemetery, riding there on Bette's bike. She had been given some lupin seeds by her Granddad, who had collected them whilst fishing, and he had told her to take them and plant them at her grandmother's grave. Bette's bike was a Hercules bike, the first one that Bette had ever owned, and she intended to have it sent to Blackpool later. Ada had previously wanted to ride it to school but her mother would not let her for fear that she would damage it.

After going along Penistone Road, Ada went over Hillfoot Bridge and rode along the side of the River Don, towards Owlerton and Wardsend cemetery. There would often be horses at the side of the river pulling coal barges. On the path, Ada encountered four cheeky young lads who decided to block her way. To get past them, she had two choices, either ride towards the river or ride towards the wall. She had no choice and rode towards the wall. Unfortunately, she hit the wall and the front wheel was buckled as she collided with it. Ada was distraught, not daring to go home and face her mother with Bette's bike in such a state.

She carried on to the cemetery, and planted all the seeds, as her Granddad had told her, and then decided to push the bike all the way to her uncle William's who lived on Butterthwaite Crescent at Shiregreen, a distance of about 4 miles. She did not know how to get there but kept asking people the way as she trundled along. Finally she arrived, but when uncle William saw the bike, he declared that he was not able to mend it but would take it back to Wigfalls in Rutland Road on his horse and cart the following day.

After he reassured Ada that it would be fixed before Bette returned from Blackpool, Ada returned home to confess to her mother what had happened. Uncle William was in the habit of calling at Percy Street every dinnertime to see the family and every day when he arrived Ada would pester him to see if the bike was mended. Eventually, Uncle William called with the bike on his cart, all mended and as good as new. He told Ada it would cost 10 bob – a lot of money then – but Ada, in tears, told him that she did not have that amount of money. Uncle William agreed to pay for it, and Ada would have to come to his house and help Aunt Rose with the household chores until the debt was cleared.

An exciting event happened whilst Bette was in Blackpool in 1934. Gracie Fields, who was one of Britain's most popular and highest paid performers, came to Blackpool to make a film called "Sing as We

Go." The Tower ballroom was used in the film and couples were selected from the crowd to appear in the film. As they danced round, they were touched on the shoulder if they were felt to be suitable and Bette was thrilled to be one of those chosen.

This photo shows Bette in the dress she wore in the film.

Filming took 3 days and Bette was paid for her services. Although the family knew Bette was in the film, and couldn't wait to go and see it, nobody was able to pick her out of the vast crowd dancing round the ballroom.

The family were always struggling to survive but food and rent were the first priorities. The rent man used to come on a Monday morning for the 6 shillings and sixpence rent. Granddad did not get his pension until Thursday, so sometimes, if the rent money was not available, Ada, usually accompanied by cousin Freddie, had to go and pay it at an agent's office in Norfolk Street, on Saturday morning.

On one occasion, in June 1934, when Ada was 14, she and Freddie were caught up in a terrifying situation. They had been to pay the rent and decided to have a walk around. As they got to Barker's Pool, they heard a band playing and saw this huge crowd. Excited, they decided to stop and take a look. They noticed that there were a group of men wearing black shirts outside the City Hall. They did not know that this was Oswald Mosley, the fascist leader, who was visiting Sheffield. The date was 28th June 1934. A branch of his party had formed in Sheffield in May 1931. Freddie wanted to go home, but Ada wanted to stay and hear the band that she felt sure were about to start playing again. They were at the back of the crowd but could just about see the police on their horses. Suddenly, trouble started, and the crowd surged. Ada and Freddie were squashed tight against a window, not being able to move and fighting for breath. They were convinced they were either going to be pushed through the window at any moment, or have the breath squeezed out of them. Eventually they managed to squirm their way out and run back down Norfolk Street and home.

In Peter Harvey's book "Sheffield in the 1930s", he states that 'at one meeting in 1934, a large crowd gathered in Barkers Pool and booed and shouted as

Mosley and his black-shirted followers marched into the hall two abreast. About 400 police were on duty around the hall and, after scuffles broke out, 6 men were detained. There was more trouble inside when Mosley's speech was interrupted, and leaflets were thrown from the grand circle. Several men were ejected by stewards."

After that, whenever Ada saw a crowd of people, she would freeze and make her way round in another direction.

Ada and Freddie also used to visit the local market regularly on a Saturday morning. The stallholders would see from the look of them both that the family had very little money and would take pity on them. They would say "Do you want a bag of fruit" and give them a bag full of damaged fruit – apples and oranges usually. The children would feel so proud as they made their way home with their great big bag of fruit for the family.

Ada left school at 14 years of age and quickly found a job at a factory on Allen Street, off Shalesmoor. This factory produced little metal typefaces, in the shape of each letter, that were used in the printing industry. Ada was instructed to fetch a container full of them and then sort them into letter As, Bs, Cs etc. and put them onto a thin stick one at a time. They were so sharp that as Ada picked them up, they cut into her fingers and made them bleed. Ada was very impressed by the speed of the other women who had been working there for years. These women were on piece-work and their fingers moved like lightning as they slotted the types onto the sticks. If anyone went past your bench and knocked into it, (sometimes on purpose) all the types would be scattered, and you would have to start again. Ada was also extremely embarrassed by the foul language of these women and only managed to put up with it for a week, before telling her Granddad that she could not bear to continue because of the painful state of her fingers. The wage she received was only about 2 shillings for the week, whereas the women who were on piece-work could earn about 30 shillings.

Ada soon found another job at Burdall's Gravy Salts, on Shalesmoor. This was back-breaking work for a young girl. Ada's job was to go along a passageway, and then down into a filthy cellar to bring up a heavy tray full of half-inch cubes of gravy salts. There was an old bloke at the machine that made the cubes, and, with an oil-can in his hand, squirted oil all over the place, not caring where the oil went, even when it went into the gravy salts. Ada made a vow never to use gravy salts again. To avoid having to go down the cellar many times, Ada and her workmates tried to carry at least 3 trays at a time, which was not easy! After getting back to her workbench, Ada then had to wrap each cube in waxed paper and put them onto a conveyor belt. The next girl would pack them into boxes, and then another girl would wrap the box. Ada was only there for a week when she received a telegram from her sister Bette, telling her that she had managed to get her a job with her at the Windsor Hotel in Blackpool, where she was the cook. Ada was so excited that she couldn't wait to leave, even telling her Granddad that he could go and pick up her wages from Burdall's!

Although Rose had sworn she would never have another baby, after losing Thelma so tragically, Rose and William were delighted to discover, in early 1935, that Rose was pregnant again and the baby was due in November.

At the end of March 1935, at Easter time, Bette was preparing to go back to the Windsor Hotel in Blackpool for her second season, this time with her younger sister Ada, who was so excited to be going with her.

There was a knock on the door and when Bette answered it, a young soldier was standing there. She did not know who he was. He said, "Don't you remember me – I'm Frank. Frank Bell." Bette answered abruptly "Oh, yes, I remember you now, but I'm in a hurry. I'm packing to go to Blackpool."

He asked if he could walk to the station with her and she agreed. He told her he was on leave for a fortnight and asked if he could come to Blackpool, so they could spend some time together. She told him that she would be working long hours and only had a couple of nights off every week, but he said he did not mind, he still wanted to come. He also showed her a photo that he had of her – it was the one she'd ripped up a few years before. He had picked every piece up and stuck it on a postcard so he could keep it with him while he was away in the army. Her embarrassed response was, "Oh my God! You've actually saved that?"

After spending time with Bette in Blackpool, he continued to write to her while he was away, and the next thing was, in the space of 7 weeks, they had decided to get married.

Ada had arrived at the Windsor Hotel at Easter 1935, a hotel owned by Mr & Mrs Young, and, as one of the two kitchen maids, was put to work with her sister Bette the cook. There were also 2 chambermaids, one of which was Ada's neighbour, Nellie Senior, and 2 waitresses, along with "Boots", a young man who cleaned any shoes that guests left outside their rooms, as well as bringing in the suitcases, dressed proudly in his green uniform.

Unfortunately, the kitchen staff received no tips, unlike the other members of staff, although they were provided with their meals. Ada's wage was 7 shillings and sixpence a week. After the guest rooms were cleaned and dinners served, the chambermaids and waitresses would have a couple of hours free, but very often the kitchen staff would still be washing up from dinner-time when it was time to get the teas ready. One of Ada's tasks, while Bette and the other kitchen maid prepared the teas, was to take little Mary Young, the daughter of the Youngs, out for a walk. Even though the weather was fine, Mary was not allowed to take her coat off, and always had to wear long woolly knee socks and shoes.

Ada and Mary in Blackpool

Bette and Frank Bell were married at Whitsuntide on Monday 10th June 1935 at the Parish Church of St John, Sheffield, with Bette wearing a second-hand wedding dress. Photos were sent to Ada in Blackpool, who was unable to get any time off to attend her sister's wedding.

Ada returned to Sheffield when the season finished at the end of October and excitedly told the family that she had been asked by Mr & Mrs Young, the owners of the Windsor Hotel in Blackpool, to go with them to their home in Crews Hill, Enfield, London. Ada was so thrilled to have been selected for work during the closed season, but Bette had even more exciting news - Ada was going to be an auntie!

Unfortunately, things were not to turn out as happily as everyone hoped.

Frank and Bette had gone to live at the home of Frank's father, Charles on Maltravers Crescent. Frank's mother had died ten years earlier, so Bette took on the role of housekeeper. One rainy day, while Frank and Bette were leaving the house, Bette slipped on one of the steps. To break her fall, she had grabbed the handrail and badly twisted herself. Not a great deal was made of this at the time, but a short while after, Bette started to complain of bad stomach pains. The doctor who attended her said that she had an upset stomach, possibly colic, and he prescribed some medicine.

Bette's pains got steadily worse, so much so that one day Frank did not go to work and sent for the doctor. The regular doctor was not available, and a young locum arrived. He asked how long Bette had been ill with stomach pains and he was told that it had started about a fortnight previously. The doctor told Frank to go to the telephone on the corner of the street and ring for an ambulance immediately as she should have been admitted to hospital sooner.

Ada, still in London, received a letter from her mother to inform her that Bette had been taken into hospital. A few days later, Ada had been to the cinema with a friend from a nearby farm at Crews Hill and as she arrived back, Mr Young was waiting for her.

He asked her, "Are you expecting any bad news from home, Ada?" Ada replied "No, but as you know, our

Bette's in hospital, but my mother told me she's all right and not to worry."

"I'm afraid you have to go home," replied Mr Young, "Bette died this afternoon. The telephone exchange has phoned a message through." The date was 17th November 1935. The hospital had been unable to save her.

Fifteen-year-old Ada refused to believe it, crying and saying, "They've sent the wrong message through – it can't be true." Collapsing in hysterics, she was comforted by Mr & Mrs Young.

The following day, Mrs Young took Ada into Enfield to order flowers and then Ada was put onto the train for Sheffield. Ada was still traumatised and as the train travelled along, she mentally said, over and over again in time to the rhythm of the train, "It can't be true, they've made a mistake, it can't be true, they've made a mistake, " fervently hoping that she could change what had happened by simply repeating those words. However, as soon as she got to the station, and saw her Granddad's face, she knew that it was true and that her beloved older sister had died.

The fall down the steps had resulted in Bette internally rupturing herself and the baby had died inside her and poisoned her. The cause of death on the death certificate was given as "Ruptured right tubal gestation."

Bette, aged just 23, was buried on 23 November 1935 at Burngreave Cemetery in the same grave as Frank's mother Mary.

Frank gave Bette's gold watch to Ada. An employer of Ada's later accused her of having either stolen the watch or received it from a boyfriend, which greatly upset Ada. Frank was devastated by Bette's death, and continued to keep in touch with the family, but did eventually remarry several years later.

Four days after Bette's funeral, on 27th November 1935, William and Rose's son, William Miles Waterfall was born. This child brought happiness back to the couple after the tragedy of losing their daughter Thelma under the hooves of a carthorse at the age of 18 months.

For the next few years, Ada would regularly return to Blackpool for the season and went to work for a Mr & Mrs Lawless who owned two houses, one for boarders and one for people who looked after themselves.
Ada loved it, working for the Lawless family, and found a good friend in Aggie, one of the girls who also worked there. Aggie came from Mexborough.

Ada is in the centre of the photo

One of Ada's duties was to prepare all the breakfasts in the morning, helped by Mr Lawless. There were two eggs for the male guests, but only one for the ladies or children, with bacon, sausage and tomatoes. The breakfasts were all put into a gigantic bain-marie, and Ada learnt from Mr Lawless that if you put the eggs in when they had just started to turn white, they would finish cooking in the bain-marie and in this way perfectly cooked eggs would be produced. She would put this knowledge to use years later when working as a cook at Rotherham Hospital.

In the other house, Mrs Lawless would cook any food that was brought in by the guests. The clients would bring in steaks, sausage etc and put their names on it, for Mrs Lawless to cook. They would then pay for the « cruet », which was a charge levied for the cooking of their own food.

Unlike at the Windsor Hotel, all the tips were pooled and saved by Mrs Lawless who would then share them out at the end of the week. Usually, wages and tips would come to about 17 shillings and sixpence each. When Mr Lawless was about, Mrs Lawless would give out a pound to the girls and, with a wink, would say « So you owe me half a crown then».

They knew she never wanted that half-crown back, and Ada and Aggie always asked Mrs Lawless to save all their tips, so that they could buy some item of clothing to wear when they went home at the end of the season.

Ada and Aggie, being such good friends, usually dressed alike, except that Aggie's skirts were much shorter than Ada's, and her make-up was more heavily applied. Ada was a quieter, more reserved person than her friend, who had quite a fiery but likeable personality.

On one occasion, at the end of September 1938, when they returned to Sheffield, Aggie was dressed in a fur fabric coat and Ada in a similar brown coat. They both had matching hats trimmed with lace, with new shoes and handbags, and some money to spare from their saved tips. As they came out of Ada's home in Percy Street, dressed up to the nines, and crossed the street, one of the neighbours who lived in the caretaker's house opposite, was talking to someone on the doorstep. As they passed, they heard the neighbour say, « It makes you wonder where they get their bloody clothes from, dun't it? » Ada was speechless, unlike Aggie who exploded! She turned around and cried «We've bloody worked for these clothes, and bloody hard too! From 5 o'clock in the morning until 12 o'clock at night! » The woman shut up, went in and slammed the door. It was a common assumption that when girls returned home, dressed decently or fashionably, that they were « on the game ».

Ada and Aggie divided their time between Ada's home and Aggie's at Mexborough. Whilst in Mexborough, they went to the Empress Ballroom, even though Ada did not know how to dance, and met up with all of Aggie's friends. When in Sheffield they went to various dance halls, including the Cutler's Hall. When their money ran out, they went to sign on at the Labour Exchange and were both sent up to Stumperlowe Mansions in the Fulwood area of Sheffield. Stumperlowe Mansions consisted of 35 flats, just off Fulwood Road, and had only been completed about 6 or 7 months previously. The flats were a joint project of about seven companies - Robson's Builders, who also built Jessop's hospital; Pearsons who supplied all the bathroom fittings, glass, and mirrors; Atkinson's who supplied the carpets, bedding and other linens; Cockaynes who supplied the furniture, and other companies who supplied electrical appliances etc.

Stumperlowe Mansions, Fulwood, Sheffield

These were considered to be luxury flats at that time with many extras not normally found in rented properties. Most of them had balconies and some even had garages attached. There was a modern automatic electric lift to every floor, and, solely for use by the residents, a restaurant on the ground floor, which would provide meals to order, and cater for dinner parties.

Each flat had a post office line for an optional telephone that had an internal line for communicating with the service department. The kitchen included a fridge and a gas cooker, and constant hot water was supplied. There was a radio and television reception point in the lounge of each flat, served by a master aerial.

There was central heating in the corridors, but not inside the flats, which had a fireplace in the lounge and a portable electric radiator. They were fully furnished and supplied with linen, cutlery, and crockery and were let under lease for a period of three years, for which a deposit was required.

The American Consul had two flats there, one for himself and his wife, and the other for his son and nanny.

Other residents included Mr Dickey, the head of Steel, Peech and Tozer, and his wife, the Haythornthwaites who were seriously involved in protecting the countryside from over-development and the host and hostess of the Grand Hotel who would organise dancing displays for the guests.

Aggie and Ada were both given employment. Aggie preferred to take employment as a cleaner, but Ada, as she was still shy and did not like meeting people, was set on in the kitchen.
They both lived in rooms in the attic as part of their employment, and there were also a few women who came in daily as cleaners.

Service kitchen at Stumperlowe Mansions

Mrs Robson, one of the directors of Stumperlowe, lived at a large house on Glossop Road and the Robsons, as well as being in the construction industry, were also involved in matters concerning the local countryside, probably as friends of the Haythornthwaites.

Mrs Robson's late husband was William George Robson who died in 1930.

The obituary in the Sheffield Telegraph stated that "*he died aged 53 after an operation. Originally from Cheltenham, he spent his early years in Newcastle and came to Sheffield about 35 years ago. He became outside manager in Longden's, the Sheffield builders and contractors, and was there for about 20 years. He set up his own business 10 years ago and had since carried out several important contracts in the city and other parts of the country. He was a prominent Freemason, being a member of the Rainham Lodge in London. His father was also a well-known builder. He leaves a widow and four daughters."*

Mrs Robson had in her employment a butler cum chauffeur, who was, in fact, a sort of carer for her, but who she treated more like a son than an employee. He would dress her, chauffeur her to various high-class functions at the Cutlers Hall, then drive her back home, usually the worse for drink, undress her and put her to bed. Mrs Robson had offered him the job of head porter and barman at Stumperlowe Mansions which he accepted.

His name was Albert Keightley, known to friends as Carl and he was to become Ada's husband.

Albert Keightley

Albert was born in 1897 to William and Millicent Keightley. In 1911 the family, including 8 children, lived at 27 Haywood Road, in the Pitsmoor area of Sheffield which would remain the family home for over 30 years.

In 1915, at the age of 18, Albert had joined the Army to serve in the First World War. He signed on for 12 years and when the war ended, he returned to Sheffield being kept on reserve until 1927.

He found employment as a tram conductor and, in 1920, married his first wife Eleanor. The marriage ended in divorce in1928.

Albert had had a variety of jobs, including salesman for John Bull, and Betterware, but was never out of work for long. One of his employments was at Speke aerodrome in Liverpool where he worked as a cook for the airmen there.

In 1938, Albert was set on as head porter/barman at Stumperlowe Mansions, on the recommendation of Mrs. Robson. Whilst working there, a new young lady joined the staff to work in the kitchen.

That young lady was Ada Bramhall, only 18 years old. Albert was 41.

Life at Stumperlowe Mansions went on, with Ada working in the kitchen along with a cook, Aggie cleaning the flats and Albert as the Head Porter and Barman. Albert also supervised another man to help him when needed. The cook's husband worked as the waiter for the restaurant, and the manageress would also help in the kitchen on occasions.

Albert would be expected to deal with any requests from the guests. The American consul might need a suit cleaning in a hurry, so Albert would arrange for it to be taken to Abbey Glen, where he had an arrangement for a speedy service. If they wanted any special liquors providing, he would manage to get them for them. Some of the residents would have visitors and wanted to provide food for them in their flats, so Albert would order a hot buffet from outside caterers. Ada would be instructed to lay out the buffet food in the private kitchen of the resident's flat, and Albert and Aggie would act as waiter and waitress for the guests. In this way, they would make a bit of extra income in the way of tips.

Albert's birth certificate does not show a middle name, but he was known to everyone as Carl. It was only Ada who called him Al.

Al had a friend who was a taxi driver, and if any of the residents wanted a taxi, he was the one that Al called, so he was a frequent visitor to the flats. One day, the taxi driver asked Aggie if she would like to go out with him,
but she felt reluctant to go alone, so she asked Ada to accompany them. Ada refused to go with them as a "gooseberry", so Aggie suggested that his friend Carl, the porter, might like to go with them. Ada was hesitant at first, saying that she did not really know him, but they eventually agreed to all go out together in the taxi.

They went to a country pub on the outskirts of Sheffield, where there was a roaring log fire and they enjoyed the evening, having a game of darts and a chat. Although the taxi driver did not drink, Al and Aggie did. Aggie drank whisky and dry ginger, but Ada, who had never been a drinker and had hardly ever set foot in a pub, thought she would play safe and just drink cider, which she thought was just a soft drink like lemonade.

As the evening wore on, Ada kept warning Aggie not to have any more to drink as they had to be up early the following morning, but Aggie carried on, telling Ada not to be silly, she was all right. For every whisky that Aggie had, Ada had a cider. When the time came to leave the pub, as soon as Ada got outside, her knees buckled under her and she had to be helped into the taxi. All the way home, they had to keep stopping for Ada to be sick at the side of the road. Aggie who had been on whisky all night was fine!

They would often all go out together after that first disaster, and Ada found that Al, as well as being very good-looking, was also good company. They then started going out on their own, with Al arranging for them to have their half days' leave at the same time. They would go into Sheffield, have a meal at Davy's or Lockwood's before going to a show at the Lyceum, and then return to Stumperlowe.

The residents all had their own kitchens, but most of them were professional people, on a good income, who preferred to eat in the restaurant, so Ada and the cook were kept very busy. There was also a bar downstairs, which Al would manage, and there were also plans in hand to have a sort of residents' club, equipped with saunas, something unheard of in those times.

The manageress had her own flat next to the kitchen and Al also had his own flat, which was more like a bed-sit. Although the manageress did not like Al and was always finding fault with something he had done, she knew that because of his close relationship with Mrs Robson, one of the main shareholders, any criticism of him was not likely to be sympathetically received.

The cook, a little fat woman, and her husband were a Cockney couple and very fond of drink.

Things came to a head on Christmas Day 1938. Many of the residents decided to have their Christmas dinner in the restaurant. The cook, helped by Ada, was preparing the dinner, and regularly swigging alcohol as the morning went on. Surprisingly, the food was very well prepared but when the cook's husband came back from the Rising Sun at Ranmoor, where he had been all morning, he was as drunk as a lord.

Al, smartly dressed in a white jacket and bow tie, had festively prepared all the tables and everything was ready for the meals to be served. The residents had taken their places at the tables. As soon as Al saw the cook's husband, who was supposed to be waiting on the tables, he knew that he was in no condition to serve any meals. But, before he could stop him, the drunken waiter appeared at the door of the restaurant and shouted, in his best cockney accent, "Nah, then, yer old bleeders! Don't you think **we** want a rest an' all? Can't yer get yer own bleeding dinners for once?

Yer've all got a bleeding good kitchen up there in yer flats!"

Al grabbed him and marched him out of the restaurant and took him to the kitchen, intending to sober him up with strong black coffee. But, when the manageress saw the state of him, she sacked him and his wife on the spot. Al went berserk, as it now rested on Ada and himself to cope with all the dinners for the residents. The food had all been cooked but the meals needed serving up. Aggie and the manageress were forced to help, but Al was livid as he was convinced that he could have sobered the waiter up with black coffee, and the manageress could have dealt with him later.

Thankfully, they managed to serve all the residents' dinners with no complaints, but it was a very hard and busy Christmas day for all of them.

From that day on, after the sacking of the cook and the waiter, Ada was on her own in the kitchen, occasionally being helped by the manageress when they were busy. It was hard work and very long days from early morning to evening. Ada would be up early, preparing breakfasts for those who had ordered them. There were also some vegetarians who wanted salads, or cauliflower cheese, and this always put extra pressure on Ada, as there had been two employees in the kitchen before, and the manageress was in no hurry to employ another cook.

One day, in the early summer of 1939, the manageress and Al had another almighty row. Al decided he had had enough and was leaving. Since he and Ada were "courting" by then, Ada decided she would leave with him, but was told that she was obliged to stay until another cook was found, so she did agree to stay for another fortnight.

Al then needed a reference to go looking for work, and, knowing that the manageress would be unlikely to provide one, he went to see Mrs Robson. Mrs Robson, who had always treated Al like a son, tore a strip off him, swearing at him and telling him that he should have come to see her about the problems he was having with the manageress. She told him to return to Stumperlowe and she would make sure he got his job back. Al dug his heels in and refused to go back.

In any case, he told her, he had seen this live-in job advertised at Lindrick Common; the only problem was that a married couple was needed. As Al and Ada had already decided to get married at Christmas that year, he thought he could persuade Ada to agree to bring the date forward so that they could apply for the job, and Mrs Robson willingly provided them with references.

Ada's mother Florence had a few reservations about Al, mainly because he was so much older than Ada, and only 4 years younger than herself. She asked Ada if she was sure that she knew what she was doing by getting married to this older man, and Ada assured her that she had no worries. Ada's Granddad, Richard, had no problem accepting Al into the family and got along very well with him from their very first meeting.

They went for the interview for the employment at Lindrick Common with a Mr Smith and his wife and discovered that the property – Birkett House - was a beautiful house at the end of a long drive, in its own grounds, opposite Lindrick Golf course. Living accommodation would be provided for them in a separate flat leading off from the kitchen. The reason that a married couple was preferred was because the property was quite a distance from Worksop, and buses were infrequent. Younger, single employees had found that as the house was in the countryside, two and a half miles from Worksop, they were not easily able to enjoy their days or nights off.

Mr Smith had a retail shop on College Street in Rotherham, which sold uniforms for waitresses, and overalls and shirts for employees. These items were made in the upstairs rooms, before selling them in the shop downstairs. The uniforms were intended for high-class restaurants and similar establishments.

Al and Ada were offered the jobs and were married on 7th August 1939. Al was a week away from reaching 42 years of age and Ada was 19.

They had a few days away for their honeymoon and spent it in Liverpool, where Al had been working before he went to work for Mrs Robson.

He had been employed at Speke aerodrome as a cook, preparing meals for the airmen. The officers' breakfasts were supposed to be of a higher standard than the ordinary airmen's, but Al, always a fighter against social injustice, made sure that all the men got the same fare, even if it meant that the officers were also served eggs as hard as bullets.

They stayed in a small bed and breakfast hotel and Al took Ada round to see all his old friends, mostly pub landlords, who were of all colours and nationalities. There was a huge Norwegian fellow in one pub, who proceeded to give Ada a big hug, lifted her off her feet and kissed her on both cheeks. Their next stop was Chinatown, home to the oldest Chinese community in Europe. Al took Ada into a little Chinese cafe cum takeaway. The Chinese owner was thrilled to see his old friend, and pulled back a bead curtain, calling all his family forward to be introduced to Al's new wife. There were about 10 children going down in steps from about 14 years old to two years old, and Ada and Al had to go down the line, shaking hands with each one, until they came to his wife at the end. She was a tiny little woman, unable to speak English, but like the rest of the family, so friendly and beaming broadly at them both.

Although Al escorted Ada around the streets and pubs, where he had many friends, he told her that it was not safe to wander around this area alone. One of the pub landlords, who had lived in the area for donkeys' years, explained to Ada that although it was a rough area, there were all nationalities getting along fine together, with the occasional argument, but becoming friends again by the following day, with all differences forgotten. It was usually strangers who caused the only real problems, foreign seamen coming off the ships, wanting to make trouble and start a fight.

Al also took Ada for a trip on the River Mersey, but to Ada's extreme embarrassment, she was as sick as a dog, asking herself how anyone could possibly suffer from seasickness on a river!

On their return from Liverpool, they went to stay for a couple of weeks with Al's youngest sister Winnie and her husband Frank Best, who lived at Firth Park. Winnie and Frank had been witnesses to their marriage.

When they went to start their new jobs, they were surprised to find that their first duties were not at the Lindrick Common house. Instead they were asked to travel to Skegness to a large holiday home that the Smiths had rented for a month. They had to get it ready for occupation by the family. There was a separate bedroom for Ada and Al. Their instructions were to clean all the carpets, air the rooms, make sure the central heating was in good working order, and stock the larder with provisions written on a list given to them by the Smiths.

The Smith family were intending to arrive on 3rd September for their holiday, but something happened that caused the cancellation of all their plans. War was declared! Al and Ada received a phone call telling them that they had to return to Worksop, as the family were no longer planning to go to Skegness. All the provisions had to be shipped back to Worksop or taken back to the suppliers.

Ada and Al then started work at the Lindrick house. The first few weeks were great, but gradually they realised that although Mr Smith was a friendly, likeable chap, always ready for a chat, his wife had an entirely different personality.

On a daily basis, Ada had to cook all the meals for the family, which were done on a great big Aga that Al also had to keep fuelled for the central heating and hot water.

Dinner parties for between 6 and 10 guests would be held regularly, with Ada and Al expected to prepare and serve the meals with no other staff to help them. With no washing machine, Ada also had to deal with all the family's washing and ironing.

The bathrooms, which were furnished with huge glass panels, had to be rubbed down every morning.

There was also a huge pine staircase that ascended from the entrance hall and this had to be cleaned every day.

A nanny was employed to look after the Smith's 6-year-old son Jimmy. He had his own nursery, and his nanny had an adjoining flat. Ada was also expected to clean the nursery and his bathroom. Ada thought that the Smiths must have expected a daughter, because the bathroom was entirely decorated in pink. Jimmy was a very spoilt child and the nanny was not expected to do any cleaning, only to devote her entire time to looking after Jimmy. She would come down to the kitchen every morning to prepare both their breakfasts. She would then take their breakfast tray back up to the nursery, after telling Ada what they wanted for lunch that day. Ada was instructed to prepare two puddings every day, so that Jimmy could choose which one he wanted.

Mr and Mrs Smith were never home for lunch, but they were always in for dinner, more often than not followed later by several guests. As a result, Ada, at the tender age of 19, was expected to prepare dinners almost daily for 10 or more people, and Al had to clean all the silver tableware before setting the table with the dinner service, cruets, and cutlery.

But Mr Smith was a lovely man! He asked Al if he liked a glass of beer. When Al said that he did, Mr Smith bought him a barrel of beer that Al kept in the cellar. Mr Smith would often come down to the kitchen to chat with Al and ask him if he could have a glass of his beer. Al would fetch him a jug from the cellar, but Mrs Smith did not approve and made her feelings known. She would say to her husband, "Drinking beer! You're not working class!" Mr Smith would ignore her and tell Al that he would still like a glass of his beer.

Ada and Al would eat after all the dinner guests had been fed, but usually there would only be the leftovers from dinner for their meal. Mrs Smith had instructed the gardener to bring in just the right amount of vegetables for dinner, so there would not be much left for Ada and Al if the guests had eaten heartily. After the dinner, Mrs Smith would come along to the kitchen and decide which food she wanted to be put into the fridge for the following day. The only food left for Ada and Al would be a few vegetables, so they would regularly walk into Worksop to buy fish and chips, even though their food was supposed to be included in their pay, which amounted to £10 a month for the two of them.

After being there a few weeks, they made the acquaintance of the outdoor staff, consisting of a gardener, a groom for the horses, and another man who looked after the dogs. These three employees told tales of how many house staff had passed through the doors in a very short time. Some of them only lasted a fortnight and it was all put down to Mrs Smith's treatment of them. Jimmy had already had 12 different nannies and he was only 6 years old! He had even had a nanny who had looked after one of the royal children, but even she had only stayed for one month.

The problem with Mrs Smith was that she had a working-class background, a miner's daughter, and she had no idea how to manage staff. She thought that she had to throw her weight around to get things done and to keep the staff firmly in their place. She would complain to Ada that she had found a crease in one of her blouses, so warned Ada to make sure that she ironed it properly next time.

On one occasion, she accused Ada of not polishing the black glass panels or the gold fittings in the bathroom. Ada replied that she had done them that morning. Mrs Smith screamed at her "Don't you answer me back!" Ada replied that she was not answering back, she was merely telling the truth and that she had rubbed them all down. Again, Mrs Smith screamed that there was condensation all over them, to which Ada replied that Mr Smith had had a shower after she had finished cleaning the bathroom. Just as Ada was still trying to explain, Mr Smith came along the passage and confirmed that he had indeed had a shower after Ada had cleaned the bathroom, but Mrs Smith just walked away without apologising for wrongly accusing Ada of not doing her chores.

Mrs Smith also liked to flaunt her wealth by regularly going down to London to buy clothes for herself and Jimmy. All the clothing had to be hand washed by Ada, and as some of them were made of silk, Ada had to be very careful. Thankfully, the bedding was sent to the laundry, but Mrs Smith then announced to Ada that she was thinking of getting a washing machine, so that Ada could wash them at home, as she complained that the sheets were hard when they came back from the laundry.

Mrs Smith would also frequently make comments to Ada about the difference in ages between her and Al, saying she could not understand how a young girl would marry a man of his age. This understandably would irritate and embarrass Ada, who thought it was none of her business. As far as Ada was concerned, she had a very happy marriage.

When Ada found out she was pregnant, she informed Mrs Smith, who had a brilliant plan for them all. She told Ada that she could continue to work for them and when the baby was born, it could go into the nursery to be looked after by the nanny. Ada and Al knew that they would never agree to that - they would be raising the child themselves, not entrusting it to the nanny and risking it becoming as spoiled as Jimmy.

One day, Al and Mrs Smith had a particularly nasty argument and Al was furious with the way that she shouted and belittled him. He told Ada to pack their things, as they were moving out, because he was not going to be talked to like a dog. He then went into the Library with a cup of coffee for Mrs Smith and told her that that was the last coffee that he would be serving her, as they were leaving immediately. Mrs Smith told them that they could be prosecuted for leaving without serving their notice, to which Al told her she could keep their final wages.

When she asked why they were going, Al told her that they were fed up of being treated so badly, surviving on a few vegetables for their meals, especially now that Ada was pregnant. Furthermore, they would be bringing up their baby themselves and had no intention of letting the nanny take over. He told her he would go and see Mr Smith in Rotherham to explain why they felt it necessary to leave and they would then be returning to Sheffield.

So they went to Rotherham to see Mr Smith. Upstairs, there were a group of girls working on the machines making the uniforms, and Mr Smith took them into his little office, where he listened to their story. After pleading with them to stay, saying that he would sort things out with Mrs Smith, he realised that they were determined to leave, and asked them if Mrs Smith had paid them what was owed to them. They informed him that they had told Mrs Smith to keep any money owed to them and they would manage, but Mr Smith gave them £20 which was 2 months' wages and wished them well for the future.

When Ada and Al returned to Sheffield from Worksop, they managed to get rooms in a house on Suffolk Road, near to Midland Station. Also living in rooms in the house were four men who worked as drag acts on the clubs. They were lovely caring men, fussing over Ada during her pregnancy, and making sure that she and Al had all that they needed, in the way of pots and pans and other household items.

One Tuesday, Ada walked up the hill to the clinic, arriving out of breath, and was examined and told that the baby had dropped into position, and that she should not travel far from home, as the baby could arrive at any time. By the time she returned home, she was ravenously hungry, and fancying some salmon for her tea. She and Al went to the corner shop and bought a tall tin of John West salmon for one and three halfpence, and a small brown Hovis, then sat down and ate the lot.

At about half past seven, after Ada finally admitted to Al that she had had niggling pains ever since she had returned from the clinic, Al started to get worried and persuaded her that it might be wise to make their way to the hospital. Despite Ada's insistence that she felt that she was not ready yet, they decided to walk all the way up to Nether Edge hospital, a distance of just over two miles. Since it was May, it was still light. On their arrival, Al told the nursing staff that Ada had had these pains all day, with Ada adamant that she thought nothing was happening yet as they weren't severe pains at all.

The nurse took Ada away to be examined, after which she handed Ada's clothes to Al and told him to return later as the baby was ready and might be born that night. Ada went to have a bath and was then taken into the maternity ward. Shortly after, her pains increased, her waters broke, and she was taken into the delivery room. Ada was now frightened, lying on the bed, and all she could think of to do, to try and distract herself from the pain, was to count the white tiles along the walls. She would start at one end but before she completed the row, the pain returned with a greater intensity, and she would lose count and have to start all over again.

In those days, there was nothing available to alleviate the labour pains, and, as she lay there, Ada remembered visiting her friend Nellie Senior when she had had her baby. This was before Ada was married, and Nellie had told her about having her baby and that she could not even remember the labour pains the next morning. Now, Ada, laying on the bed, kept saying to herself, "Just wait till I get out of here and see Nellie Senior, she was lying! I'll never forget these pains, never!"

As Ada continued with her labour, she was comforted by Nurse Farmer at her bedside, who had beautiful big brown eyes and fat rosy cheeks. Ada was hoping that her child would also have lovely eyes just like Nurse Farmer's.

Her daughter Ann was born at 7 o'clock the next morning, Wednesday 8th May 1940. Ada told Nurse Farmer that all she could remember about having her baby was these lovely brown eyes looking down at her and reassuring her. Needless to say, Nurse Farmer was thrilled and flattered when she heard this. Ada soon forgot her pain and realised that her friend Nellie had been right.

Al had returned to the hospital the previous night, but he had been sent away and told to return the next day. He arrived at about 11 o'clock that morning and was absolutely thrilled to see his baby daughter.

So, nine months and one day after getting married, Ada and Al had their first child. Ada had been a total innocent before her marriage. When she was in Blackpool, the Black Watch band were playing in the town, and one of the girls, Aggie's cousin, went out with quite a few of them. Aggie confided that her cousin used to go onto the sands with them, but Ada could not believe that they would actually get up to anything. She had always said that she would get pregnant straight away if she ever did anything like that, and so she never did and was a virgin when she married. She was proved right by getting pregnant with Ann as soon as she got married.

Ada stayed in hospital for 3 weeks, a normal practice in those days. She had been knitting for her baby continuously since finding out she was pregnant, and she asked Al to bring up her latest piece of knitting so that she could finish it. The nurses were intrigued to note that baby Ann would always manage to get her hands out of her blanket and would be moving them about in front of her face. The nurses told Ada that the baby was imitating her mother's actions whilst she was pregnant.

When Ann was a few months old, Al and Ada decided to go for a walk up to the Crookes area to see Al's brother Doug. He was a year older than Al and they had always been close, even working together as conductors on the Sheffield trams.

Both on back row - Albert third from left - Doug third from right

Ada had never met Doug before as he had won about £20,000 on the football pools a few years previously and moved to Yarmouth where he bought a pub. Later he sold it and moved back to Sheffield. After walking up to Crookes to see him and his wife Ethel, they did not get a very good reception, being kept talking on the doorstep for about 10 minutes before they were invited in. Ada had Ann sitting on her knee and Ethel finally made them a cup of tea and produced a plate of biscuits. When Ada nervously looked at Al, she noticed that he had a piece of cotton protruding from his fly. She managed to make him aware of it by furtive looks and gestures, and he started to wrap it round his fingers. But he couldn't get rid of it, there was so much of it, but finally he got to the end of it and put it in his pocket.

When they had finished their tea and biscuits, Doug's wife Ethel immediately went out of the room and returned with a handbrush and dustpan and started to clean up, even though Ada could not see any fallen crumbs. They decided to leave, and as soon as they stood up, Ethel jumped up and began fluffing the cushions up! When they got outside, Ada turned to Al and told him never to take her there again. "Don't worry," said Al, "you're not the only one that's never going there again. I didn't know she was like that!"

They had a good laugh, however, when they returned home. When Al removed his trousers, they discovered that the piece of cotton that he had pulled at for so long, had unravelled his underpants into two separate pieces that just hung from the waistband. Ada stitched them back together the next day, as they could not afford to just throw them away.

A few weeks later, they moved a short distance from Suffolk Road to Granville Road, into a much larger bed-sit in a larger house. Ada happily settled in, especially pleased with the French windows that opened out into a garden as she was able to put Ann outside in her pram.

Al had now managed to find employment as a barman/cellarman working for Duncan Gilmours at a pub at the bottom of Duke Street, on the corner near the market.

Although the bed-sit was a nice room, and Ada kept it very clean and tidy, it was still a bed-sit, and there were some problems with the other people who shared the house. Two women and half a dozen children, who had been bombed out of their London homes, and evacuated to Sheffield, had recently moved in. But they were very dirty and never did any washing until the landlady noticed huge piles of dirty laundry piling up in their room and told them to deal with it. After a few weeks of further problems, the landlady eventually had enough of their dirty habits and told them they had to leave.

So, for this and other reasons, Ada and Al desperately wanted a place of their own, rather than a bed-sit. One day, the manager of a carpet warehouse, who was a regular in the pub where Al worked, happened to mention that he owned some houses. Al asked him if he had any vacant ones, and if not, would he keep him in mind for any that became available. One day in November 1940, he came into the pub to offer Al a house to rent, but the key had to be bought for a sum of £20. Since Al was only earning £2 a week at that time, £20 was a lot of money, and Ada was bitterly disappointed, fearing that they would never be able to manage to find that amount to secure the house. But Al managed to borrow the money from a friend and they therefore became the proud tenants of their own house at the bottom of St Mary's Road, near to Midland Station. Their daughter Ann was nearly 7 months old.

The house was not large but felt to be big enough for the three of them. There was a kitchen/living room with a sink, one bedroom upstairs, and a further bedroom up another flight of stairs, three rooms in total. Most houses at that time also had a cellar. They went to the sale rooms and bought a bed, a dining room suite, consisting of a sideboard, table and 4 chairs, a little half-moon rug, and a companion set for the coal fire.

Ada's mother bought curtains for the three windows in the house as she had not yet had chance to buy them a wedding present, and other members of the family bought them other necessary items such as pans and crockery. Ada went to the local Woolworths and bought some glasses that were made in Czechoslovakia. All the glasses were sixpence each, whether they were whisky glasses, liqueur glasses or half pint glasses, so Ada bought six of each. She left all her purchases safely wrapped up in a cardboard box until she had decided where to put them. All the shelves in the kitchen needed freshly papering, which is something that was done in those days.

Ada set to work and cleaned all the little sash windows in the kitchen, bedroom and attic bedroom and when Al came home from work, he helped to put the curtains up. They were so pleased with their first proper home and the new curtains looked lovely.

Three weeks after they moved in, events took a serious turn. By 6 o'clock, Ann was fast asleep as usual, in her cot upstairs. Ada could hear bombing noises in the distance, and as they got louder and louder, despite Al's advice to leave Ann a bit longer as it would probably pass over, she decided to bundle her up in her blankets, still asleep, and fetch her downstairs. There was an Anderson shelter outside, but as they had only just moved in, they had not had the time to inspect it properly. Some of these shelters regularly filled up with water, so Al decided that they would be better off going down into the cellar. They took with them some candles and a peg rug, given to Ada by her mother. At the bottom of the cellar steps, there was a stone table on which food was stored to keep it cool. After placing the peg rug under the stone table, Ada placed Ann on the rug without waking her, and sat down on the cellar steps, with Al sitting at her side on a kitchen chair, the only light coming from a few candles.

The noise of the bombing got steadily worse and the red alert sounded at 7 p.m. The house was near to Midland Station, and the arches near the station were used as stables for the carthorses belonging to Duncan Gilmours. One of the most upsetting sounds that they heard whilst sitting there, was the distressed screams of the terrified horses which were now running loose on the cobblestones as they frantically tried to get away from the bombing around them.

Ada was petrified by now and Al did his best to comfort her. When Ann woke as usual at 9 o'clock for a feed, Ada discovered that, due to her absolute terror, her breast milk had drained away. She wondered what they were going to do, as by now they had no water left, and there was no milk in the house. Al disappeared upstairs and returned with half a bottle of rum and half a bottle of black beer. These were mixed together and given to Ann on a teaspoon. At first Ann spit the mixture out, but Al told

Ada to persevere, saying that if Ann was not going to survive, she would be better to die without feeling anything, in other words by being senselessly drunk. Ann started to take it, and eventually fell asleep.

Al then tried to persuade Ada to drink some as well, but Ada could not stomach it after a few spoonfuls. As they sat there, the sound of the bombs got louder and louder, some of them whistling as they came down. Whilst Al went upstairs for something, Ada suddenly heard a deafening, whistling sound. As she shouted for Al, the explosion and blast from the bomb threw her back onto the steps where she cracked her head, causing a wound that bled, but which did not knock her out. Ada was in a lot of pain from this whiplash injury. She had given up smoking as soon as she found out she was pregnant, but now, crying and being reassured by Al that it would all be over soon, she told him that she would be able to calm her nerves if only she had a cigarette. Al, who had smoked all of his Players by now, finally decided that they were not staying in the cellar to be buried alive, they were going outside.

The time was half past two in the morning, and as they went up the cellar steps, they felt as though they were walking on a thick carpet. They did not know it at the time, but the "carpet" was actually a thick layer of soot and debris. When they emerged outside, with Ann bundled up in a blanket, there was a brilliant full moon and as they looked across the street, they could see all the houses opposite with no roofs or windows. Ada turned to Al and said, "Oh those poor people, look at their houses!" But when they turned around, they were devastated to find that their house was in exactly the same condition, with Ada's brand-new curtains in shreds and blowing in the wind.

They scrambled out of the yard and everywhere they looked, there were no buildings left standing. As they walked along the road, they came to a little club that Al knew might have some cigarettes. As he hammered on the door, under which they could see a chink of light, the landlord appeared, shouting, "Nah then, Carl, what's tha' doing out here? Why dunt tha' get thissen inside?'" "We've been inside for long enough, and we're not staying there to get buried alive!" was Al's response, ignoring the cries of the wardens shouting to them to get off the street.

After explaining to the landlord that all they wanted was a "packet of cigs" to calm their nerves, they were given a packet of Park Drives. Then, with Ada in her coat and slippers, and Ann still tightly wrapped in a blanket, they made their way towards Haywood Road at Pitsmoor, where Al's parents lived. They picked their way along Duke Street, then Commercial Street, and arrived at Fitzalan Square. Ada would remember forever the sight that greeted them – she recalled that it was like Dante's Inferno – a Spencer Tracy film she had seen in 1935. Nearly every shop, hotel and building was on fire, including the seven storey Marples hotel, and the large C & A store. But, remarkably, now that she was in the open air, Ada was no longer afraid.

They made their way to the top of Commercial Street, and then walked down Haymarket, where there were all sorts of large stores, that had been severely damaged, including Woolworths and a big jewellers' shop. They gazed in horror on seeing bodies strewn all over the place but laughed with relief when they realised that they were fully clothed mannequins that had been blown out of the department stores.

There were air raid wardens directing them as to the best way to go, and as they walked along, they were up to their knees in water. As they reached the bottom of Haymarket, the all-clear sounded. The time was half past four in the morning.

Ada sighed with relief, knowing that no more planes would be coming over, and no more bombs would be dropped for the time being. Cold and weary, they made their way towards the Wicker but were turned back by the wardens as the Wicker arches had received a direct hit. As they diverted along Nursery Street to the bottom of Corporation Street, and then towards the railway, they heard the sound of planes coming over. They crouched down at the side of a great big six-foot wall until the planes had passed over, then went along Rock Street up to Haywood Road. As they walked along, they saw that most of the houses had no roofs or windows, but luckily, these were not on fire like the ones in the centre of Sheffield.

When they arrived at Al's parents, William and Millicent, they found them sitting there terrified, with no windows in the house. Millicent had always refused to go into the shelter, and tonight was no exception. Al set to work with some old blankets, nailing them up to the windows to keep out the bitterly cold night. As they made a cup of tea, Ada asked if there were any old sheets she could use to change Ann's nappy, which had not been changed for such a long time after leaving their bombed-out house.

As she unwrapped Ann from her blanket, Ada let out an almighty scream. Al came running in, thinking his daughter was injured. Ada was able to see Ann's face clearly for the first time since they had left their home, and saw a little black face looking up at her with only the whites of her eyes visible. Ada thought she was covered in bruises but was relieved to find that it was only a coating of soot, and that she was totally unharmed. There was no water supply to the house, but, using a flannel and a little bit of water from the kettle, Ada managed to clean her up slightly, after which she promptly fell back to sleep – more than likely still drunk from the rum and black beer.

In any case, there was nothing in the house to feed a baby, apart from some tinned milk, which Ada did not think would be suitable. Al suggested that, if she woke up, they could give her some more of the rum and black beer that he still had in his pocket, but Ada refused, fearing that they might end up killing her. As it was, Ann did not wake up again until 11 o'clock the next morning, probably with a hangover!

After deciding that they had better now go and see if Ada's family were all right, they made another cup of tea for Al's parents, put plenty of coal on the fire, fetching another bucket up from the cellar, thereby making sure that they would be warm enough until they were able to return.

They made their way down the back of Haywood Road, down a steep hill and through Bingley and its shops, via Harvest Lane, Nursery Street, onto Burton Road and eventually arriving at Percy Street.

Although all the windows had been blown out of the houses on Percy Street, there had been no fires. Ada's Granddad went to fill the great big iron kettle to put it onto the fire to boil the water for a cup of tea, when suddenly there was an almighty roar of an aeroplane going over the house. Granddad, terrified, and still clutching the kettle, ran for the cellar and managed to get himself wedged between the kitchen table and the cellar door. Everyone burst out laughing as Al reassured the family that "it's only one of ours going back to base" and Granddad, feeling slightly foolish, had to agree that our planes did have a different sound to the enemy ones, whilst extricating himself. The sound of laughter relieved all the tension that everyone felt after a night of being bombed and scared to death.

Ada's mum found a piece of towelling so that, even though Ann was still fast asleep, her nappy could be changed. They all had a cup of tea, and after making sure everyone was all right, Ada and Al returned to his parents on Haywood Road.

The next day, the council arrived and "billeted" Ada and Al on his parents, as there was no room for them at Percy Street. An allowance would be paid to William and Millicent for Ada and Al to stay with them. The only problem was that Millicent and William, now in their seventies, had not slept together for over 20 years, so Al had to sleep with his dad in the front bedroom, and Ada had to sleep with her mother-in-law in the back bedroom, with Ann at her side in a wash basket for a cot. Ann was uncomfortable in the wash basket, and started to wake up during the night, something that she had not done for months. Ada fed her on rice pudding to start with, but after 3 days, Ada's breast-milk returned and she was able to start breast-feeding again.

There was still a major problem, however. Ada would try to avoid waking her mother-in-law during the night as she fed her daughter but would not get much sleep herself because Millicent was an early riser. She would get up between half past three and four o'clock every single morning.

Monday was washday. Everything was prepared the night before. Millicent sorted out the washing and William chopped all the sticks and placed them under the copper boiler, ready for lighting the next morning. He would also put a bucket of coal ready at the side. The washing would be completed and hung out in the communal yard before any of the neighbours rose from their beds.

Millicent was a fantastic cook, and she would prepare the dinner, usually some sort of stew in a casserole dish in the oven, and then go back to bed for a few hours. Ada felt obliged to get up and help her with these early morning tasks, but she herself could not go back to bed as Ann would then be awake and ready for washing and dressing.

The dinner, cooked to perfection by the time Millicent got up, was served at exactly 12 noon. As Al was working at Duncan Gilmour's and the pub did not close until 3 p.m., his dinner was put between two plates in the oven until he came home.

Thursday was baking day. Again, Millicent was up at half-past three, baking bread, teacakes and scones, before going back to bed.

Friday was black-leading day, which meant that black lead (or graphite) was applied to the fireplace or stove to clean it. Once again, Ada was up at the same time as Millicent to help her to do the chores. Millicent would then go back to bed, leaving Ada to deal with Ann who would be awake by about half past seven.

William and Millicent would go to bed about 9 o'clock, but Ada would not go to bed until about midnight after waiting up to give Al his supper after he had finished work. The pubs closed at 10 o'clock, and after clearing up, Al would have to walk home, arriving at about 11 o'clock. One night, when Al came home, Ada was fast asleep in an easy chair, and no supper had been prepared. Al wanted to know why she was always so tired, and she explained that she had been getting up with Millicent at the crack of dawn every day to help with the chores. Al was livid. He had thought that when he got up in the morning from his father's bedroom, Ada had only just got up. He shouted upstairs for both William and Millicent to come downstairs. When he asked them why Ada was having to get up early every morning, Millicent responded by saying "Well, I never asked her to!" Al told them both in no uncertain terms that Ada would not be doing that in future, and furthermore, he and Ada were now going to be using the front bedroom, and William and Millicent were going to have to share the back bedroom. After all, they were getting paid for them being there.

Ada was happy that Al had now sorted out the problem but was nevertheless determined that Millicent would have no reason to criticise her for not getting up early to help with the chores, so she took all her dirty washing, including the bedding, to her mother's house at Percy Street.

The German bombers were still targeting Sheffield and the air raid sirens would regularly be heard in the Sheffield industrial areas. Millicent was a very stern, intimidating woman and Ada was slightly frightened of her, being only 20 years old. Al was usually at work during the evenings so was not around to face up to his mother. Millicent would refuse to go into the shelter when the sirens sounded. She also ordered Ada to stay in the house, even though Ada wanted to go and fetch Ann downstairs and go into the shelter. "Don't you go disturbing that babby! Leave her where she is!" she would shout.

One Sunday night, the bombing was particularly bad, and Ada was terrified. She decided she had to make a stand. She jumped from her chair, shouting, "Bugger you! I'm fetching her downstairs!" She had never sworn before in her life, but she was determined that she was not going to stay indoors and be bombed. She went and lifted Ann out of the wash basket and ran out of the front door.

Mr White, the next-door neighbour, was coming down the street at the time, and he was an air-raid warden. "Where do you think you're going?" he shouted to Ada.   "Anywhere! Anywhere!" replied Ada, visibly upset.

Mr White calmed Ada down, saying, "Come with me into our shelter, I'll take you." The shelter was in the cellar and had been strengthened with concrete by the government. Mr White told Ada "Take no notice of your in-laws, let them stay in the house if they want. Come and join us in the shelter whenever you want."
Now in the shelter, Ada calmed down and felt safe, not being able to hear a sound whilst in there, even though bombs were dropped in the Attercliffe area that night.

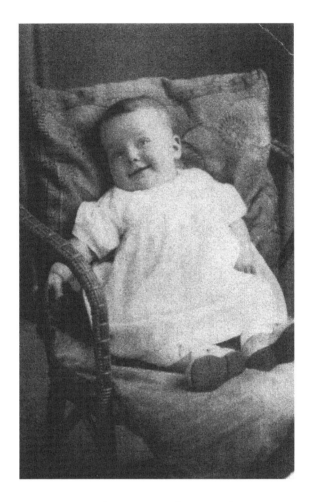

Ann age 6 months

One day, in 1941, Al's boss at Duncan Gilmour's sent for him. Duncan Gilmour's was a Scottish company, with strange principles. The founder never employed an Englishman in an English pub, or a Scottish man in a Scottish pub, but no-one quite knew why. His pubs never opened on a Sunday, as he would say that if he could not brew enough beer for his customers to drink in 6 days, then he was not interested in supplying enough for them to drink in seven.

On this occasion, the previous procedures were not followed, because Al was offered the job of manager of a pub in Rotherham. Al was definitely interested, but the only drawback was that there was no living accommodation provided. Ada was adamant that she was not going to Rotherham to live in rooms again, but Al persuaded her to go and have a look at the pub.

The pub was the Kings Arms on the corner of Doncaster Gate and College Street and known as "Dunks". The previous manager had left and there were two barmaids there, sisters Annie and Mary Rogerson. They told Al that the former manager had been frequently absent for no known reason, and they themselves had been running the pub, and were even in possession of the keys. After looking round, Ada and Al left the pub, with Al declaring to Ada that if he decided to accept the job as manager, there was no way the barmaids would retain control of the keys, as he knew he personally would be held responsible for the stock.

Al's boss had suggested that they should go to Cox, Dewar and Beaton's, a local estate agent at the Crofts in Rotherham, to see if they had any houses to let. Al and Ada, with Ann in her arms, went there and were told that there was only one house on their books at the present time. They were warned that it was in a filthy state and the address was number 14

Upper Clara Street, off Psalters Lane. They said they would go and have a look at it, and were offered a lift in the manager's car, a rare treat for them as nobody had cars in those days.

The house was even filthier than they had imagined! The red brick quarry tiles on the kitchen floor were all broken; there were 2 bedrooms, and a living room, a little pantry and a backyard. Knowing that Al had his heart set on taking over the pub, Ada said, "Well it's gonna need some cleaning, but I'll do it!"
"Are you sure?" said Al, to which Ada replied that she was not going into rooms again, and she would definitely take on the task of getting this house cleaned up.

Ada spent 6 weeks travelling between Rotherham and Sheffield every day, costing her threepence a time on the tram. Duncan Gilmours had brought Ann's pram and a few pots and pans from Sheffield, so that Ada could put Ann to sleep and make herself a cup of tea and a gas cooker was ordered from the gas showrooms.

In the cellar, Ada found a great big drum of a liquid that looked like black tar. Al told her it was creosote, and someone told her that it could be used to kill any bugs in the house. Ada painted all the walls, skirting boards, and floorboards with it. Cockroaches began to emerge out of the walls and skirting boards and Ada shovelled the bodies up every day. Gradually they became fewer and fewer and smaller and smaller until they were all disposed of. Ada then papered the living room and whitewashed the bedrooms before stippling them with different coloured paint.

Ada and Al went to the sale-rooms in Sheffield and bought a three-piece suite made of hide for £5. Their dining room suite that they had bought for their first house had been left out in two lots of snow after the Sheffield blitz as all the storage rooms were packed out because of the number of people who had suffered bomb damage. Ada and Al had luckily managed to cover the suite with blankets and it was still in a decent condition. No items had been stolen from their bombed-out house. Everyone was in the same boat and rallied round to help each other to get back to normal.

Duncan Gilmours then brought all their belongings to Rotherham on a lorry, the driver complimenting them on the bargain they had got with their good solid hide three-piece suite for a fiver.

Ada had also bought some wall plates at the salerooms, which depicted a seaside scene, with an old man telling a story to two little boys sitting on an upturned boat. Ada had wrapped these treasures carefully in a blanket, but the driver did not balance them properly on the table and they fell off and smashed to bits on the tile floor. Fortunately, he was more careful with her box of Woolworth's glasses.

Because they had been bombed out of their house in Sheffield, they had to go to an office on Moorgate to make a report of all they had lost in the blitz, and they would then be helped to replace essential items. They received the grand total of £6, with a promise that they would be given some more when the war ended.

Since they only had 2 cups and 2 mugs, and no pans, Ada bought some pots and pans. When they were bombed, Ann's cot had escaped damage, but bricks and rubble had landed on their bed.

Al had already repainted Ann's cot and for their first night in their new home, they had reassembled their bed and made it up with fresh sheets and blankets. As soon as they got into bed, however, the bed collapsed. It had a wooden headboard and a wooden bottom that were held together by iron struts. The iron had cracked due to the bomb blasts and finally broke when they got into bed. They had to sleep on the mattress on the floor for quite a few weeks until they could afford to go to the salerooms and buy another bed.

When Al was offered the job as manager of "Dunks", he told Mary and Annie Rogerson that in future he would have control of the keys for the pub, as he was responsible for all the stock, and that he would be the first to arrive in the morning. This did not go down too well with the Rogerson sisters, who had been used to running the pub and felt they were being downgraded.

A stock-take was done by the brewery prior to Al starting, and a new barmaid, Mrs Pycroft, was set on at the same time as Al. A few days later, Al was told by one of the regular customers that on the day before Al took over, and after the stock-take, the Rogerson sisters, who had decided that they were going to leave, had been giving all the customers free drinks. They had taken exception to Al because they had been working at Dunks for several years and were used to being in charge. They were telling all the customers "Drink up lads, the drinks are on Duncan Gilmours. We'll show him, the clever bugger, he's not taking the keys off us, after we've been here all these years." The oldest sister, Mary, had also been the "cellarman", connecting all the barrels, and tapping them.

Al, knowing that he would be held responsible for any deficit in the stock, decided that he would immediately call in the stock-takers again, after reporting to Duncan Gilmours what had happened. It was confirmed that the stock was down by a significant amount and the sisters were invited to leave.

A few days later, Annie, the younger sister returned and apologised to Al, blaming her sister Mary for the trouble they had caused, and asking if she could have her job back. Although she was an alcoholic, Al relented but stressed that she was on trial and could not behave as she had in the past. Al had already set on another young barmaid, but she had been called to go and work in a munitions factory. As Mrs Pycroft, the new barmaid, was an older lady, and not likely to be called for wartime duties, Al asked Duncan Gilmours if he could have another man to work with him as a barman/cellarman, and a little chap with a moustache by the name of Jack Russell was employed.

He and Al got on like a house on fire and he reminded Ada of her granddad. Jack and Al would regularly sit and have a game of dominoes when the pub had closed.

Annie was more of a problem. She was an alcoholic and was always drunk. She liked her rum but did not always pay for it! Al would tell her that she could have the occasional drink, which he could cover by getting 3 drinks out of a bottle that was only intended to provide 2. They had a rule that there could be no bottles in the best side, so it was easy to make a bottle spin out to 3 drinks. In the taproom, he could not make anything up on the drinks, because the customer was given the bottle. So, he had to keep a really good eye on the stock.

The pub was always busy, especially on a Monday, because it was market day and the miners always had Mondays off. Dunks was the only pub in Rotherham that had plenty of liquors, because they received their stock, not in bottles, but in 1 gallon and 2-gallon jars. They also dealt in black market items, something that frightened and embarrassed Ada, but apparently, everyone was doing it.

There was a NAAFI next door and one of the soldiers used to fetch in great big joints of pork and beef. He would park his bike in the passage at the back of the pub, which led into the smoke room or into the best side, and coming into the pub, would say to Al, "Can I have a packet of Park Drives?" This was the signal to let Al know that there was a parcel on his bike. Al would give the soldier a fiver with his packet of cigs and go and collect the parcel. Ada and Mrs Pycroft would then take it down to the cellar and cut it in half to share it.

Al used to say that the passage at the back of the pub would be ideal for churchgoers to use if they wanted a crafty drink, because if they disappeared down the passage, no-one would know they were going into the pub.

Mrs Pycroft also knew someone who used to kill his own pigs, which was allowed at that time. But the pork had to be declared and was subject to rationing. Mrs Pycroft would get a whole leg of pork on the quiet and would share it with Ada. One week Ada would have the knuckle end, with the best section going to Mrs Pycroft and the next week Ada would get the best bit.

The manager of the Meadow grocery shop would receive a big case of bars of soap, but not enough to give one to each of his customers, so he would offer it for sale to Al. As Al walked along with the case of soap on his shoulder, Ada would be terrified that he would be stopped by the police and land himself in trouble. Eventually, they had to tell the soldier to stop bringing the meat because he was bringing it faster than they could use it, even though they would make sandwiches for the customers in the pub. Ada was not used to lying and would go beetroot red whenever she was asked where the meat had come from. Other soldiers would bring in slices of ham, a cucumber, some salad or fresh fruit or vegetables, and swap them for a packet of cigarettes.

Ada and Al now moved from Upper Clara Street to a rented house next door to Mrs Pycroft, their barmaid. This was number 7 Lindum Terrace, on Doncaster Road, opposite Clifton Park, and was to be their home for the next 30 years, with three more children being born there.

A recent photograph of 7 Lindum Terrace. The three-storey house has now been converted into 3 privately owned flats.

Al's father, William died on 21st February 1943, aged 76, and was buried at Burngreave Cemetery, Sheffield.
A month later, Al and Ada's second child Anthony Carl William (known as Tony) was born on 17th March.

Ann & Tony

Ada's Granddad, Richard Waterfall died on 25th June 1944 at the age of 71.

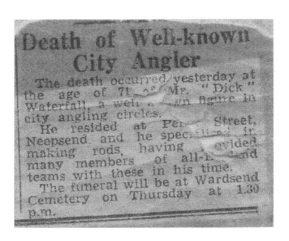

> ## Death of Well-known City Angler
>
> The death occurred yesterday at the age of 71 of Mr. "Dick" Waterfall, a well . . . . wn figure in city angling circles.
>
> He resided at Pen . . . Street, Neepsend and he spec . . . . ir making rods, having . . . . vided many members of all-l . . . nd teams with these in his time.
>
> The funeral will be at Wardsend Cemetery on Thursday at 1.30 p.m.

Grandad Richard was a fat, jolly little red-faced man who, to amuse the children, would wiggle his ears, making a wart on his forehead move up and down. Everyone remembered him as a lovely man, so kind and patient and mourned his passing.

He was buried in Wardsend cemetery in the same grave as his wife Annie and granddaughter Thelma.

He had spent many an hour at the grave at Wardsend after Annie and Thelma died, sitting on the slope looking at the views all around Sheffield. The graveyard was covered in lupins, thanks to Ada having scattered the seeds around her Grandmother's grave in 1933 at her Grandad's request.

Following Richard's death, his daughters Florence and Rose went to Frank Bell's house to tell him that Granddad Richard had died. Frank had been so close to the family when his late wife Bette was alive but had since remarried. Frank and his wife welcomed them in. They were amazed and deeply touched to see that the photo of Bette, which the young soldier Frank had stuck together all those years ago, had been enlarged, put into a photo frame and was displayed on the living room wall. His wife, who had known and been a friend of Bette's when they were children, declared that they would never part with that photo, as Bette had been a very special person.

In 1945, a second tragedy struck Rose and William Waterfall who had lost their toddler Thelma in 1933 under the hooves of a carthorse. Rose took their young son William, aged 9, on a week's holiday to Southport near Liverpool. His father William was away from home in the army.
William had never been on holiday before and was so excited by his first sight of the sea.

William Miles Waterfall and his mother Rose

Towards the end of the week, after paddling and swimming in the sea, young William cut the instep of his left foot on some broken glass on the beach and was taken to the local hospital, where it was cleaned and bandaged.

They were due to return to Sheffield the next day, so Rose was advised to take him along to Sheffield hospital to have it dressed, which she did.

A few weeks later, William started complaining that his legs were aching. Everyone put this down to "growing pains" but when his pains continued, Rose took him to the doctor's whose opinion was that he was a growing lad and these pains were common and nothing to worry about.

When the pains spread to William's back and he was unable to get up from the settee, Rose, who had some days off work, sent for the doctor. The doctor diagnosed "a thorough cold which was in his bones, not in his head."

William's condition worsened, so much so that Rose had to carry him to the toilet, as he was unable to walk. She sent for the doctor again, who this time diagnosed pneumonia and prescribed M & B tablets to be taken every two hours, and he would arrange for William to be admitted to hospital.

These were the days prior to antibiotics being available and, for serious infections, including pneumonia, M & B tablets were given – these initials stood for the manufacturer May and Baker.

Meanwhile, Rose had received a telegram from her husband William who was a Corporal in the Yorkshire and Lancashire Regiment. He had been in Italy and was on his way home. For reasons of security, he was not allowed to say when he would arrive, so Rose asked the doctor if young William could stay at home that day in case his father arrived, and she would continue to give William the prescribed M & B tablets. The doctor agreed but said that an ambulance would collect William the following day.

William senior arrived at 2 o'clock in the morning and was devastated to see the condition of his young son. He had promised William a bike when he returned from the army and one of young William's first questions to his dad was "Am I going to have my bike now, Dad?" "Of course you are son," said his Dad, "as soon as you're better, we'll go down and get one."

The next morning the ambulance arrived to take William to hospital. In those days, parents were not allowed to stay with their children, so, at about 11 o'clock, after William had been settled in, Rose and William were told that there was no need to wait, William would be all right, and the hospital would be in touch if necessary.
At about half past three that afternoon, a policeman arrived to ask Rose and William to return to the hospital as their son William was very ill. By the time they got to the hospital, William had died.

An inquest was held which determined that although penicillin (a new drug recently developed) had been used to try and save him, a microbe had entered the cut that he had suffered on the beach.

The death certificate gave the cause of death as "Cardiac exhaustion from Tetanic convulsions following cut on instep of left foot. Cut accidentally sustained whilst playing on sands at seaside."

He was buried in Shiregreen cemetery.

Following this tragic death of a second beloved child, Rose nearly had a nervous breakdown, and everyone feared that she would be admitted to a mental hospital, had it not been for the love and support of her husband William.

The whole family was once again engulfed in grief and, from that time on, Rose and William seemed to close into one another and were never apart.

With William's discharge grant and the money Rose had managed to save from her earnings, they bought a little greengrocer's shop near Percy Street and then in Page Hall. Rose worked in the shop and William bought a van and sold his fruit and vegetables around the Shiregreen and Firth Park areas of Sheffield, eventually buying a little wholesale business. So, even though William had had hardly any schooling, he made a decent living. All their strength and time went into this enterprise as a way of coping with their grief. They never had any more children, or got over their loss, and remained close until the day they died.

On 7th August 1990, Rose died. Not surprisingly, William collapsed and died 5 days later, and they were buried in a joint funeral service in the same grave as their beloved son William.
On the return from the funeral, the family were disgusted and horrified to find that a long solid mahogany sideboard had been stolen from the house, along with some gold sovereigns that belonged to Rose.

Al continued as manager at Duncan Gilmour's for a few more years, but then went to work at the Alma Road Workhouse as a hospital orderly.

With 2 small children, Ada could not go out to work, but another opportunity arose for her to supplement the family income.

Mrs Pycroft, who lived next door at number 6 Lindum Terrace, used to take in boarders, and asked Ada if she wanted to do the same, by making use of the large house with attic, in which the Keightley family lived. Ada thought she would give it a go, and the first boarders she took in were young Polish lads that had been referred to her by Mrs Pycroft, who had no vacancies at that time. The lads were full board and Ada even packed up sandwiches for them and did their washing and ironing.

These lads worked for a firm called Walshams who erected and maintained pylons. A van would pick them up and take them to wherever they were working. When they moved to another area, Walshams would pay Ada a retainer to keep their rooms for when they had to return to the Rotherham area to do repairs.

In the interim period, Ada would offer bed and breakfasts, usually men coming to Steel, Peech and Tozers for one day to do repairs. They would only stay one night, before working all day at "Steelo's" and then returning home. She would receive a letter from Walshams, about 2 weeks in advance, asking her to confirm that she could be ready to accommodate several of their workers, and by just doing bed and breakfast in the interim period, she could get their rooms ready in good time. The lads would share a large bedroom, or the attic, usually three to a room and were well looked after.

The Polish lads were like members of the family, because they came back time and time again. Julian was a little fat chap who had many skills, such as cobbling shoes, and he also mended Ada's chairs. He married a Polish woman from Oldham who had 2 children. He would go home every weekend but would bring any of the children's shoes and sandals back with him that needed mending so that he could repair them during the week. Ada was fascinated to see him unpick the complete shoe, remove the crepe sole, replace it and stitch it all back together again with a leather sole. Sadly, when the lads returned on one occasion, Julian was not with them. He had been up one of the pylons with a huge roll of wire when one of the ends had unravelled and wrapped itself around him, severely injuring him. He was in hospital for a very long time and never worked again.

Another lad was Frank Racing, who, although Polish, was born in France. He used to darn his own and the other lads' socks, as well as doing their ironing. Some of the lads were German Poles who had escaped from Germany and joined the Polish Air Force.

Ada was happy with her boarders, as they were a lovely clean group and she had very few problems with any of them.

Al also had a German friend who used to come and visit on occasions, but it is not known how they came to be friends.

In 1946, Ada had another burden to bear, in the shape of her mother-in-law, Millicent, now aged 75, who was still living at Haywood Road. Her neighbour Mr White, the former air-raid warden, heard a loud banging and when he went round to investigate, discovered that she had fallen. He knew that Al lived in Rotherham, but not the exact address, so he got in touch with Doris, Al's younger sister, who then got in touch with Winnie, the youngest daughter in the family. Neither of them had spoken to their mother for twenty years, for reasons unknown. It was clear that Millicent was no longer able to live alone. Doris immediately declared that she could not look after her, as she was working, although it was later discovered that it was only part-time, with a husband and son also out at work. No-one else felt able to offer to have her, so Al and Ada agreed that she could come and live with them.

Al hired a taxi with a roof rack and they fetched everything she needed from her bedroom from Haywood Road - her bed and bedding, her bedroom carpet, a photo of her baby Cecil who had died at a few months old, some items of china, and a few trinkets. She was installed in the back bedroom upstairs. Doris told them that she would sort out and dispose of everything in the rented house at Haywood Road and bring the proceeds to her mother. It was a five-roomed house that was fully furnished with some good quality items. There was bedroom furniture in the front bedroom, the back bedroom and the attic, four dining chairs and two matching easy chairs upholstered in the same material, a chaise longue, a large settee, a huge kitchen table, a piano, a sewing machine, and all her crockery, pots and pans. Doris sold them all at an auction house and sent Millicent a bank book with the grand sum of £8 in it! Millicent was heartbroken and furious.

Al found out where the auction house was and discovered that Doris had only put a few of the items through the auction in Millicent's name, but the more valuable items had been put through in her own name. Even though she was not well, Millicent decided to take Doris to court. Although Millicent had no proof that all the items were hers, having owned them for years, the court realised that the other items were antiques, and concluded that they were more likely to have belonged to Millicent, not Doris. The court ordered Doris to pay Millicent another £40.

Millicent was a very opinionated person and not easy to look after. For her keep, she gave Ada the £2 10 shillings a week that she got from her late husband's pension and kept her own 30 shillings pension for herself.
She loved sweets and Ada would buy her a mixture from Kenworthy's in Rotherham market. But she was so greedy and would stuff a handful at a time into her mouth, prompting Ada to warn her that she risked choking herself to death. Another thing she did was to try and cadge the children's sweets from them, but she never did it in Ada's presence. The children did not get many sweets, but they would come into the kitchen to complain to their Mum that Grandma was asking them for their sweets, even though she had her own supply in her large white apron pocket that she always wore over her dress.

Another annoying thing that she did occurred every time that Ada was baking. Ada would take out a tray of jam tarts from the oven, and, as soon as her back was turned, Millicent would immediately take two of the red-hot tarts and quickly put them into her apron pocket, thinking that Ada would not notice that they had been stolen. Ada would repeatedly tell her that she could have them with a cup of tea when they had cooled down, but Millicent still insisted on stealing them.

She then became incontinent and had to be moved into the downstairs back room. She would never leave her chair or tell Ada that she needed the toilet. But, like Little Britain's Andy character, she could move when she wanted to, especially to turn the Redifusion radio switch off when Ada went to hang out the washing. Since there was no television in those days, Ada loved listening to the radio while she worked, so she would get really annoyed with Millicent.
Another child, Karen, was born on 17th June 1947.

Shortly after, Al moved on from his job at the workhouse, and found new employment at Robert Jenkins, a large boilerworks on Wortley Road.

Seventeen months later, on 15th November 1948, son John arrived. If he had arrived a day earlier, on the same day that Prince Charles was born, he would have received a commemorative food gift parcel, which would have been gratefully received as food rationing was still in force until 1954.

It was not a well-paid job at Jenkins and Ada had had to cut down on the number of boarders she could take in, due to Millicent taking up a room, and needing a great amount of care. She also needed a fire in her room which stretched the family's finances, as Ada and Al now had 4 children from ages 1 to 9, and life could be tough.

Karen & John – born in 1947 & 1948

None of Millicent's family came to see her, except on one occasion when the family was really struggling. Al had written to his sisters Ethel, who lived in Yarmouth, and Winnie, who was still in Sheffield, to see if they could help with the cost of keeping the fire going in Millicent's bedroom. There was no reply from Winnie, but Ethel came to see them and gave them enough money for a ton of coke. After staying a couple of days, she returned to her family in Yarmouth.

After suffering three strokes, Millicent died on 30th November 1949 and was buried at Moorgate cemetery, Rotherham.

Following this sad event, Ada was once again able to increase the number of boarders that she catered for, and although living continued to be difficult at times, with four children to raise, she never lost her kind and loving personality, willing to help anyone who needed it.

To be continued?????

Printed by Amazon Italia Logistica S.r.l.
Torrazza Piemonte (TO), Italy